Wit without Money. A comedie ... Written by F. Beamount [sic], and J. Flecher, Gent. [or rather, by Fletcher alone].

Francis Beaumont

Wit without Money. A comedie ... Written by F. Beamount [sic], and J. Flecher, Gent. [or rather, by Fletcher alone].
Beaumont, Francis
British Library, Historical Print Editions
British Library
1639
4°.
Ashley 91.

The BiblioLife Network

This project was made possible in part by the BiblioLife Network (BLN), a project aimed at addressing some of the huge challenges facing book preservationists around the world. The BLN includes libraries, library networks, archives, subject matter experts, online communities and library service providers. We believe every book ever published should be available as a high-quality print reproduction; printed on- demand anywhere in the world. This insures the ongoing accessibility of the content and helps generate sustainable revenue for the libraries and organizations that work to preserve these important materials.

The following book is in the "public domain" and represents an authentic reproduction of the text as printed by the original publisher. While we have attempted to accurately maintain the integrity of the original work, there are sometimes problems with the original book or micro-film from which the books were digitized. This can result in minor errors in reproduction. Possible imperfections include missing and blurred pages, poor pictures, markings and other reproduction issues beyond our control. Because this work is culturally important, we have made it available as part of our commitment to protecting, preserving, and promoting the world's literature.

GUIDE TO FOLD-OUTS, MAPS and OVERSIZED IMAGES

In an online database, page images do not need to conform to the size restrictions found in a printed book. When converting these images back into a printed bound book, the page sizes are standardized in ways that maintain the detail of the original. For large images, such as fold-out maps, the original page image is split into two or more pages.

Guidelines used to determine the split of oversize pages:

- Some images are split vertically; large images require vertical and horizontal splits.
- For horizontal splits, the content is split left to right.
- For vertical splits, the content is split from top to bottom.
- For both vertical and horizontal splits, the image is processed from top left to bottom right.

643.g.21.

Beaumont & Fletcher

Wit without Money

edit. 1639.

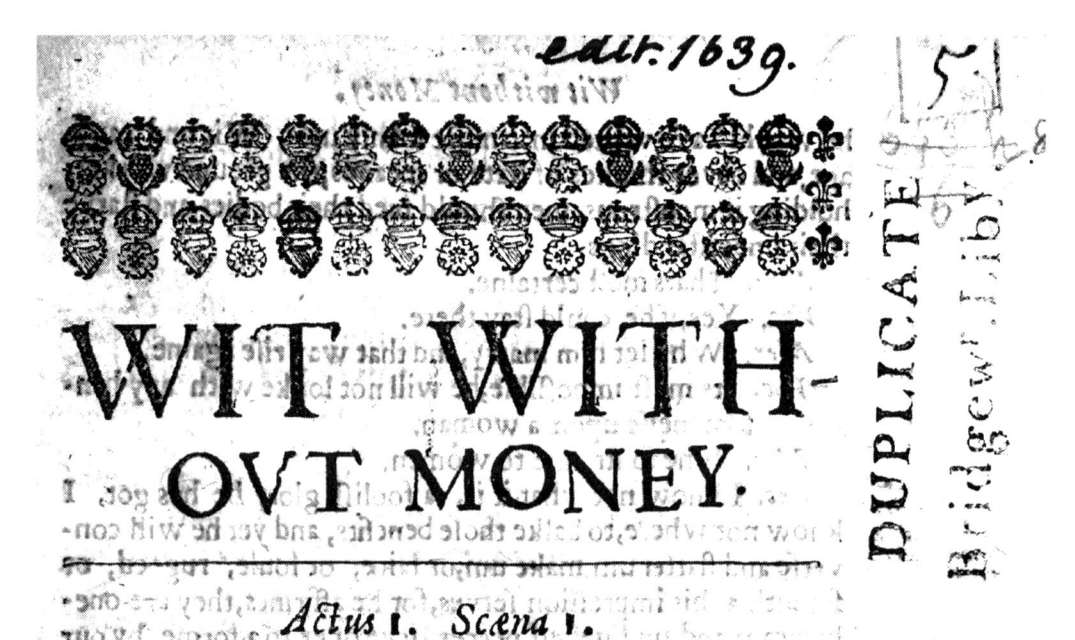

WIT WITH-OVT MONEY.

Actus 1. Scæna 1.

Enter Vncle and Merchant.

Merchant.

When saw you *Vallentine*.
Uncle. Not since the Horserace, he's taken up
with those that wooe the Widdow.
Mer. How can he live by snatches from such
people, he bore a worthy minde.
Unc. Alas, he's sunke, his meanes are gone, he wants, and
which is worse,
Takes a delight in doing so.
Mer. Thats strange.
Unc. Runs Lunaticke, if you but talk of states, he cannot be
brought now he has spent his owne, to thinke theres inheritance, or meanes, but all a common riches, all men bound to be
his Bailiffes:
Mer: This is something dangerous.
Unc. No Gent. that has estate to use, it in keeping house, or
followers, for those wayes he cries against, for eating sins, dull
surfets, cramming of serving men, mustering of beggers, maintaine hospitals for Kites, and curs, grounding their fat faithes
upon old Countrey proverbes, God blesse the founders; these

B   he

Wit without Money.

he would have vented into more manly uses, Wit and carriage, and never thinkes of state, or meanes, the ground workes: holding it monstrous, men should feed their bodies, and starve their understandings.

Mer. Thats most certaine.

Vnc. Yes, if he could stay there.

Mer. Why let him marry, and that way rise againe.

Vnc. Its most impossible, he will not looke with any hansomenesse upon a woman.

Mer. Is he so strange to women.

Vnc. I know not what it is, a foolish glory he has got, I know not where, to balke those benefits, and yet he will converse and flatter um, make um, or faire, or foule, rugged, or smooth, as his impression serves, for he affirmes, they are onely lumps, and undigested peeces, lickt over to a forme, by our affections, and then they show: The lovers let um passe.

Enter Fount. Bella. Haire.

Mer. He might be one, he carries as much promise; they are wondrous merry.

Vnc. O their hopes are high sir.

Fount. Is *Vallentine* come to Towne.

Bella. Last night I heard.

Fou. We misse him monstrously in our directions, for this Widdow, is as stately, and as crafty, and stands I warrant you.

Haire. Let her stand sure, she falls before us else, come lets goe seeke *Vallentine*.

Mer. This Widdow seemes a gallant:

Vnc. A goodly woman, and to her hansomnesse she beares her state, reserved, and great Fortune has made her Mistresse of a full meanes, and well she knowes to use it.

Mer. I would *Vallentine* had her.

Vnc. Theres no hope of that Sir.

Mer. A that condition, he had his morgage in againe.

Vnc. I would he had.

Mer. Seeke meanes, and see what Ile doe, however let the money be paid in, I never sought a Gentlemans undoing, nor eate the bread of other mens vexations, the morgage shall be rendred backe, take time for't, you told me of another brothers

Vnc.

Wit without Money.

Unc. Yes sir, more miserable then he, for he has eate him, and drunke him up, a handsome Gentleman, and a fine Scholler.

Enter three tennants.

Mer. What are these?

Unc. The tennants, th'ie doe what they can,

Mer. It is well prepared, be earnest honest friends and loud upon him, he is deafe to his owne good.

Lance. We meane to tell him part of our mindes, an't please (you.

Mer. Doe, and doe it home, and in what my care may helpe, or my perswasions when we meete next.

Unc. Doe but perswade him fairely; and for your money, mine, and these mens thankes too, and what we can be able:

Mer. Y are most honest, you shall finde me no lesse, and so I leave you, prosper your businesse my friends. *Exit Merchant*

Unc. Pray heaven it may sir:

Lance. Nay if hee will be mad, Ile be mad with him, and tell him that Ile not spare him, his Father kept good meate, good drinke, good fellowes, good hawkes, good hounds, and bid his neighbours welcome; kept him too, and supplyed his prodigality, yet kept his state still, must wee turne Tennants now, after we have lived under the race of Gentry, and maintaind good yeomantry, to some of the City, to a great shoulder of Mutton, and a Custard, and have our state turned into Cabbidge Gardens, must it be so:

Unc. You must be milder to him.

Lance. Thats as he makes his game:

Unc. Intreate him lovingly, and make him feele:

Lance. Ile pinch him to the bones else.

Vallen. Within. And tell the Gentleman, Ile be with him presently, say I want money too, I must not faile boy.

Lance. Youle want clothes, I hope.

Enter Vallentine:

Vall. Bid the young Courtier repaire to me anon, Ile reade to him.

Unc. He comes, be diligent, but not too rugged, start him, but afright him not.

Vall. Phew are you there?

Wit without Money.

Vnc. We come to see you Nephew, be not angry;

Val. Why doe you dogge me thus, with these strange people, why all the world shall never make me rich more, nor master of these troubles.

Tennants. We beseech you for our poore childrens sake.

Val. Who bid you get um; have you not thrashing worke enough, but children must be banged out oth' sheafe too, other men with all their delicates, and healthfull diets, can get but winde egges: you with a clove of garlicke a peece of cheese would breake a saw, and sowre milke, and I must maintaine these tumblers.

Lance. You ought to maintaine us, wee have maintained you, and when you slept provided for you; who bought the silke you weare, I thinke our labours; reckon, youle find it so: who found your horses perpetuall pots of ale, maintain'd your Tavernes, and who extold you in the halfe crowne boxes, where you might sit and muster all the beauties, wee had no hand in these, no we are puppies: Your tennants base vexations.

Vall. Very well sir.

Lance. Had you land, and honest men to serve your purposes, honest, and faithfull, and will you run away from um, betray your selfe, and your poore tribe to misery; morgage all us, like old cloakes; where will you hunt next, you had a thousand acres, faire and open: The Kings bench is enclosed, thers no good riding, the Counter is full of thornes and brakes, take heed sir, and bogges, youle quickly finde what broth they're made of.

Val. Y are short and pithie.

Lance They say y are a fine Gentleman, and excellent judgment, they report you have a wit; keepe your selfe out oth raine and take your Cloake with you, which by interpretation is your state sir or I shall thinke your fame belyed you, you have money and may have meanes.

Val. I prethee leave prating, does my good lye within thy braine to further, or my undoing in thy pitty: goe, goe, get you home, there whistle to your horses, and let them edifie, away, sow hempe, and hang your selves withall, what

am

am I to you, or you to me; am I your Landlord puppies?

Unc. This is uncivill.

Val. More unmercifull you, to vex me with these bacon broth and puddings, they a'e the walking shapes of all my sorrowes:

3. Tennants. Your Fathers Worship, would have used us better.

Val. My Fathers worship, was a foole.

Lance. Hey, hey boyes, old *Vallentine* ifaith, the old boy still.

Unc. Fie Cosen.

Val. I meane besotted to his state, he had never left mee the misery of so much meanes else, which till I sold was a meere meagrome to me: If you will talke, turne out these tenements, they are as killing to my nature Vncle, as water to a feaver.

Lance. We will goe, but it is like Rammes to come againe the stronger, and you shall keepe your state:

Val. Thou lyest, I will not.

Lance. Sweete sir, thou lyest, thou shalt, and so good morrow. *Exeunt Tennants.*

Val. This was my man, and of a noble breeding, now to your businesse Vncle.

Unc. To your state then.

Val. Tis gone, and I am glad on't, name it no more, tis that I pray against, and heaven has heard mee, I tell you sir, I am more fearefull of it, I meane of thinking of more lands, or livings, then sickely men are travelling a Sundaies, for being queld with Carryers out upon't *caveat emptor*, let the foole out sweat it that thinkes he has got a catch on't.

Unc. This is madnesse to be a willfull begger.

Val. I am mad then and so I meane to be, will that content you, how bravely now I live, how jocund, how neare the first inheritance, without feares, how free from title troubles.

Unc. And from meanes too.

Val. Meanes, why all good men's my meanes, my wits my plow, the Townes my stock, Tavernes my standing house, and all the world knowes theres no want, all Gentlemen that

Wit without Money.

love society, love me; all purses that wit and pleasure opens, are my Tennants; every mans clothes fit me, the next faire lodging, is but my next remoove, and when I please to remoove; and when I please to be more eminent, and take the aire, a peece, is levied, and a Coach prepared, and I goe I care not whether, what neede state here.

Vnc. But say these meanes were honest, will they last sir.

Val. Far longer then your jerkin, and weare fairer, should I take ought of you, tis true, I beg'd now, or which is worse then that, I stole a kindnesse, and which is worst of all, I lost my way int, your mindes enclosed, nothing lies open nobly, your very thoughts are hid, that worke on nothing but daily sweate, and trouble: were my way so full of dirt as this, tis true I shifted; are my acquaintance Grasiers: but sir, know no man that I am allyed too, in my living, but makes it equal, whether his owne use, or my necessity pull first, nor is this forc'd, but the meere quallity and poysure of goodnesse, and doe you thinke I venter nothing equall.

Vnc. You pose me Cosen.

Val. Whats my knowledge Vncle, ist not worth money, whats my understanding, my travell, reading, wit, all these digested, my daily making men, some to speake, that too much flegme had frozen up, some other that spoke too much to hold their peace, and put their tongues to pensions, some to weare their clothes, and some to keepe um, these are nothing Vncle; besides these wayes, to teach the way of nature, a manly love, community to all that are deservers, not examining how much, or whats done for them, tis wicked, and such a one like you, chewes his thoughts double, making um onely food for his repentance.

Enter two servants.

1. *Ser.* This cloake and hat sir, and my Masters love.

Val. Commend's to thy Master, and take that, and leave um at my lodging.

1. *Ser.* I shall doe it sir.

Val. I doe not thinke of these things:

2. *Ser.* Please you sir, I have gold here for you.

Val. Give it me, drinke that and commend me to thy Master,

ster, looke you Vncle, doe I begge these:

Vnc. No sure tis your worth sir.

Val. Tis like enough, but pray satisfie me, are not these wayes as honest as persecuting the starved inheritance, with musty Corne, the very rats were faine to run away from, or selling rotten wood by the pound, like spices, which Gentlemen doe after burne by th ounces, doe not I know your way of feeding beasts, with graines, and windy stuffe, to blow up butchers, your racking pastures, that have eaten up as many singing Shepherds, and their issues, as *Andaluzia* breedes; these are authentique, I tell you sir, I would not change wayes with you, unlesse it were to sell your state, that houre, and if it were possible to spend it then too, for all your Beanes in *Rumville*, now you know me.

Vnc. I would you knew your selfe, but since you are growne such a strange enemy, to all that fits you, give mee leave to make your brothers fortune.

Val. How?

Vnc. From your morgage, which yet you may recover; Ile finde the meanes.

Val. Pray save your labour sir, my brother and my selfe, will runne one fortune, and I thinke what I hold a meere vexation, cannot be safe from him, I love him better, he has wit at will, the world has meanes, hee shall live without this tricke of state, we are heires both, and all the world before us.

Vnc. My last offer, and then I am gone.

Val. What ist, and then Ile answer.

Vnc. What thinke you of a Wife yet to restore you, and tell me seriously without these trifles.

Val. And you can finde one, that can please my fancy, you shall not finde me stubborne.

Vnc. Speake your woman.

Val. One without eyes, that is selfe commendations, for when they finde they are hansome, they are unholsome, one without eares, not giving time to flatterers, for shee that heares her selfe commended, wavers, and points men out a way to make um wicked, one without substance of her selfe,

that

Wit without Money.

that woman without the pleasure of her life, thats wanton, though she be young, forgetting it, though faire, making her glasse the eyes of honest men, not her owne admiration, all her ends obedience, all her houres new blessings, if there may be such a woman.

Vnc. Yes there may be.

Val. And without state too.

Vnc. You are disposed to trifle, well, fare you well sir, when you want me next, youle seeke me out a better sence.

Val. Farewell Vncle, and as you love your estate, let not me heare on't.

Vnc. It shall not trouble you, Ile watch him still, And when his friends fall of, then I end his will.   *Exit.*

Enter Isabella, and Luce.

Luce. I know the cause of all this sadnesse now, your sister has ingrost all the brave lovers.

Isab. Shee has wherewithall, much good may doe her, prethee speake softly, we are open to mens eares:

Luce. Feare not, we are safe, we may see all that passe, heare all, and make our selves merry with their language, and yet stand undiscovered, bee not melancholly, you are as faire as shee.

Isab. Who I, I thanke you, I am as haste ordain'd mee, a thing flubberd, my sister is a goodly portly Lady, a woman of a presence, she spreads satten, as the Kings ships doe canvas, every where she may spare me her misen, and her bonnets strike her maine petticoate, and yet outsaile me, I am a Carvell to her.

Luce. But a tight one:

Isab. She is excellent, well built too.

Luce. And yet shees old.

Isab. Shee never saw above one voyage *Luce*, and credit me after another, her hull will serve againe, and a right good Merchant, shee plaies and sings too, dances and discourses, comes very neere essaies a pretty poet, begins to piddle with Phylosophie, a subtill Chimicke wench, and can extract the spirit of mens estates, she has the light before her, and cannot misse her choice, for me tis reason, I waite my meane fortune.

Luce

Wit without Money.

Luce. You are so bashfull.

Isab. It is not at first word up and ride, thou art cosend, that would shew mad I faith, besides, wee lose the meane part of our polliticke government, if we become provokers, then wee are faire, and fit for mens imbraces, when like townes, they lie before us ages, yet not carried, hold out their strongest batteries, then compound too with the losse of honour, and march oft withour faire wedding: Colours flying, who are these?

Enter Franc. and Lance.

Luce. I know not, nor I care not.

Isab. Prethee peace then, a well bult Gentleman.

Luce. But poorely thatcht.

Lance. Has he devoured you to?

Fran. Has gulped me downe *Lance*.

Lance. Left you no meanes to study.

Fran. Not a farthing: dispatcht my poore annuity I thanke him, heres all the hope I have left, one bare ten shillings.

Lan. You are fit for great mens services.

Fran. I am fit, but who'le take me, thus mens miseries are now accounted staines in their natures, I have travelled, and I have studded long, observed all kingdomes, know all the promises of Art and manners, yet that I am not bold, nor cannot flatter, I shall not thrive, all these are but vaine Studdies, art thou so rich as to get me a lodging *Lance*.

Lan. Ile sell the titles of my house else, my Horse, my Hawke, nay death Ile pawne my wife: Oh Mr. *Francis*, that I should see your Fathers house fall thus.

Isab. An honest fellow.

Lan. Your Fathers house, that fed me, that bred up all my (name.

Isab. A gratefull fellow.

Lan. And fall by.

Fran. Peace, I know you are angry *Lance*, but I must not heare with whom, he is my brother, and though he hold him slight my most deare brother: A gentleman excepting some few rubbes, he were too excellent to live here else, fraughted as deepe with noble and brave parts, issues of a noble and manly spirit as any he alive, I must not heare you, though I am am miserable, and he made me so, yet still he is my brother, still I love him, and to that tye of blood linke my affections.

Isab. A noble nature, dost thou know him *Luce*?

Luce. No Mistresse.

Isab. Thou shouldest ever know such good men, what a faire body and a mind, are married there together; did he not say he wanted.

Luce. Whats that to you?

Isab. Tis true, but tis great pitty.

Luce. How she changes, ten thousand more than he, as handsome men too.

Isab. Tis like enough, but as I live, this Gentleman among ten thousand thousand, is there no knowing him; why should he want? fellowes of no merit, slight and puft soules, that walke like shadowes, by leaving no print of what they are, or poise, let them complaine.

Luce. Her colour changes strangely.

Isab. This man was made, to mark his wants to waken us, alas poore Gentleman, but will that fledge him, keepe him from cold, beleeve me he is well bred, and cannot be but of a noble linnage, mark him, and marke him well.

Luce. 'Is a hansome man.

Isab. The sweetnesse of his suffrance sets him off, O *Luce*, but whether goe I.

Luce. You cannot hide it.

Isa. I would he had what I can spare.

Luce. Tis charitable.

Lance. Come sir, Ile see you lodged, you have tied my tongue fast, Ile steale before you want, tis but a hanging.

Isab. Thats a good fellow too, an honest fellow, why, this would move a stone, I must needes know; but that some other time.   *Exit Lance, and Fran.*

Luce. Is the winde there? that makes for me.

Isab. Come, I forgot a businesse.

Actus

Wit without Money.

Actus 2. *Scæna* 1.

Enter Widdow and Luce.

Wid. MY sister, and a woman of so base a pitty, what was the fellow?

Luce. Why an ordinary man Madam.

Wid. Poore?

Luce. Poore enough, and no man knowes from whence neither.

Wed. What could she see?

Luce. Onely his misery, for else she might behold a hundred handsumer.

Wid. Did she change much?

Luce. Extreamely, when he spoke, and then her pitty like an Orator, I feare her love framed such a commendation, and followed it so farre, as made me wonder.

Wid. Is she so hot, or such a want of lovers, that shee must doate upon afflictions: why do's shee not goe romage all the Prisons, and there bestow her youth, bewray her wantonnesse, and flie her honour, common both to beggery; did she speake to him?

Luce. No, hee saw us not, but ever since, she hath beene mainely troubled.

Wid. Was he young?

Luce. Yes young enough.

Wid. And looked he like a gentleman.

Luce. Like such a Gentleman, would pawne ten oathes for twelve pence.

Wid. My sister, and sinke basely; this must not be, do's she use meanes to know him?

Luce. Yes Madam, and has employed a Squire called *Shorthose.*

Wid. O thats a precious Knave, keepe all this private, but still be neere her lodging; *Luce* what you can gather by any meanes, let me understand, Ile stoppe her heate, and turne her charitie another way, to blesse her selfe first, be still close to

C 2   her

her Councells, a begger and a stranger, therés a blessednesse, Ile none of that, I have a toy yet sister, shall tell you this is foule, and make you find it, and for your paines take you the last gowne I wore, this makes me mad, but I shall force a remedy.

Enter Fountaine, Bellamore, Harebraine, Vallentine.

Foun. Sirra, we have so lookt thee, and long'd for thee, this Widdow is the strangest thing, the stateliest, and stands so much upon her excellencies.

Bella. She has put us off this moneth now, for an answer.

Hare. No man must visit her, nor looke upon her, not say good morrow nor good even, till thats past.

Vall. She has found what dough you are made of, and so kneads you, are you good at nothing, but these aftergames, I have told you often enough what things they are, what precious things, these widdowes. *Hare.* If we had um.

Val. Why the devill has not craft enough to woe um, there be three kindes of fooles, marke this note gentlemen, marke it, and understand it.

Fount. Well, goe forward.

Val. An Innocent, a Knave foole, a foole politicke: the last of which are lovers, widdow lovers.

Bella. Will you allow no Fortune?

Val. No such blind one.

Fount. We gave you reasons, why twas needfull for us.

Val. As you are those fooles, I did allow those reasons, but as my Schollers and companions damn'd um, doe you know what it is to wooe a widdow, answer me coolely now, and understandingly.

Hare. Why to lie with her, and to enjoy her wealth.

Val. Why there you are fooles still, craftie to catch your selves, pure politicke fooles, I lookt for such an answer, once more I eare me it is to wed a widdow, to be doubted mainely, whether the state you have be yours or no, are those old bootes you ride in, marke me, widdowes are long extents in Law upon necves, livings upon their bodies winding sheetes, they that enjoy um, lie but with dead mens monuments, and beget onely their owne ill Epitaphs, Is not this

plaine

plaine now?

Bel. Plaine spoken.

Val. And plaine truth, but if you'le needes doe things of danger, doe but loose your selves, not any part concernes your understandings, for then you are Meacockes fooles, and miserable march of a maine, within an inch of a Furcug, turne me oth' toe like a Weathercocke, kill every day a Sergeant for a twelve moneth, robbe the Exchequor, and burne all the roules, and these will make a shew.

Hare. And these are trifles.

Val. Considered to a Widdow, emptie nothing, for here you venture but your persons, there the varnish of your persons, your discretions, why tis a monstrous thing to marry at all, especially as now tis made, me thinkes a man, an understanding man, is more wise to me, and of a nobler tie, than all these trinkets, what doe we get by women, but our senses, which is the rankest part about us satisfied, and when thats done what are we? Crest falne cowards, what benefite can children be, but charges and disobedience, whats the love they render at one and twentie yeares; I pray die father, when they are young, they are like bells rung backwards, nothing but noise, and giddinesse, and come to yeares once, there droppes a sonne, byth' sword in's Mistresses quarrell, a great joy to his parents: a daughter ripe too, growes high and lustie in her blood, must have a heating, runnes away with a supple hand Servingman, his twentie nobles spent, takes to a trade, and learnes to spinne mens haire off; theres another, and most are of this nature, will you marry?

Fount. For my part yes, for any doubt I feele yet.

Val. And this same Widdow?

Fount. If I may, and me thinkes, how ever you are pleased to dispute these dangers, such a warme match, and for you sir, were not hurtfull.

Val. Not halfe so killing as for you, for mee shee cannot with all the Art shee has, make mee more miserable, or much more fortunate, I have no state left, a benefit that none of you can bragge of, and theres the Antidote against a Widdow, nothing to lose, but that my soule inherits,

inherits, which shee can neither law nor claw away to that, but little flesh, it were too much else; and that unholsome too, it were too rich else; and to all this contempt of what shee do's J can laugh at her teares, neglect her angers, heare her without a faith, so pitty her as if shee were a traytor, moane her person, but deadly hate her pride; if you could doe these, and had but this discretion and like fortune, it were but an equall venture.

Fount. This is mallice.

Val. When shee lies with your land, and not with you, growes great with joyntures, and is brought to bed with all the state you have, you'le finde this certaine; but is it come to passe you must marry, is there no buffe will hold you.

Bel. Grant it be so.

Val. Then chuse the tamer evill, take a maide, a maide not worth a penny; make her yours, knead her, and mould her yours, a maide worth nothing, theres a vertuous spell, in that word nothing; a maide makes conscience of halfe a crowne a weeke for pinnes and puppits, a maide content with one Coach and two horses, not falling out because they are not matches; with one man satisfied, with one raine guided, with one faith, one content, one bed, aged shee makes the wife, preserves the fame and issue; a Widdow is a Christmas box that sweepes all.

Fount. Yet all this cannot sinke us.

Val. You are my friends, and al my loving friends, I spend your money, yet I deserve it too, you are my friendes still, I ride your horses, when I want I sell um; I eate your meate, helpe to weare her linnen, sometimes I make you drunke, and then you seale, for which Ile doe you this commoditie, be ruled, and let me try her, I will discover her, the truth is, I will never leave to trouble her, till I see through her, then if I finde her worthy.

Hare. This was our meaning *Valentine.*

Val. Tis done then, I must want nothing.

Hare. Nothing but the woman.

Val. No jealousie, for when I marry, the devill must be wiser than I take him, and the flesh foolisher, comes lets to dinner,

Wit without Money.

dinner, and when I am well whetted with wine, have at her.
Exeunt.

Enter Isabella and Luce.

Isa. But art thou sure.
Luce. No surer then I heard.
Hare. That it was that flouting fellowes brother.
Luce. Yes, *Shorthose* told me so.
Hare. He did search out the truth.
Luce. It seemes he did.
Hare. Prethee *Luce*, call him hether, if he be no worse, I never repent my pitty, now sirra, what was he wee sent you after, the Gentleman ith blacke.

Enter Shorthose.

Short. Ith torne blacke.
Isa. Yes, the same sir.
Short. What would your Worship with him.
Isa. Why my worship would know his name, and what he is.
Short. 'Is nothing, he is a man, and yet he is no man.
Isa. You must needes play the foole.
Short. Tis my profession.
Isa. How is he a man, and no man.
Short. Hees a begger, onely the signe of a man, the bush puld downe, which showes the house stands emptie.
Isa. Whats his calling?
Short. They call him begger:
Isa. Whats his kindred:
Short. Beggers.
Isa. His worth.
Short. A learned begger, a poore Scholler:
Isa. How does he live.
Short. Like wormes, he eates old Bookes.
Isa. Is *Vallentine* his brother.
Short. His begging brother.
Isa. What may his name be?
Short. *Orson.*
Isa. Leave your fooling.
Short. You had as good say, leave your living.

Isa.

Wit without Money.

Isa. Once more tell me his name directly:

Short. Ile be hangd first, unlesse I heare him Christned, but I can tell what foolish people call him.

Isa. What?

Short. Franscisco.

Isa. Where lies this learning sir?

Short. In *Paules* Church yard forsooth.

Isa. I meane that Gentleman, foole.

Short. O that foole, hee lies in loose sheetes every where, thats no where.

Luce. You have gleand since you came to *London*, in the Countrey *Shorthose*, you were an arrant foole, a dull cold coxcombe, here every Taverne teaches you, the pint pot has so belaboured you, with wit, your brave acquaintance that gives you ale, so fortified your mazard, that now theres no talking to you.

Isa. Is much improved, a fellow, a fine discourser.

Short. I hope so, I have not waited at the taile of wit so long to be an asse.

Luce. But say now *Shorthose*, my Lady should remoove into the Countrie.

Short. I had as leeve she should remoove to heaven, and as soone I would undertake to follow her.

Luce. Where no old Charnico is, nor no Anchoves, nor Master such a one, to meete at the Rose, and bring my Lady such a ones chiefe Chambermaide.

Isa. No bouncing healths to this brave Lad, deare *Shorthose*, nor downe oth knees to that illustrious Lady.

Luce. No fidles, nor no lusty noyse of drawer, carry this pottle to my father, *Shorthose*.

Isa. No playes, nor gally foistes, no strange Embassadors to runne and wonder at, till thou beest oyle, and then come home againe, and lye bith Legend.

Luce. Say she should goe.

Short. If I say so, Ile bee hangd first, or if I thought shee would goe:

Luce. What?

Short. I would goe with her.

Luce.

Luce. But *Shorthose,* where by heart is:

Isa. Doe not fright him.

Luce. By this hand Mistris tis a noyse, a loud one too, and from her owne mouth, presently to be gone too, but why, or to what end?

Short. May not a man dye first, sheele give him so much time.

Isa. Gone oth' sudden; thou dost but jest, shee must not mocke the Gentlemen.

Luce. She has put them off a moneth, they dare not see her, beleeve me Mistris, what I heare I tell you.

Isa. Is this true wench, gone on so short a warning, what tricke is this, she never told me of it, it must not be: sirra, attend me presently, you know I have beene a carefull friend unto you, attend me in the hall, and next be faithfull, cry not, we shall not goe.

Short. Her Coach may cracke.   *Exeunt.*

Enter Vallentine, Francisco, and Lance.

Val. Which way to live, how darest thou come to towne, to aske such an idle question.

Fran. Me thinkes tis necessary, unlesse you could restore that annuity you have tippled up in Tavernes:

Val. Where hast thou beene, and how brought up *Fransisco,* that thou talkest thus out of *France,* thou wert a pretty fellow, and of a hansome knowledge; who has spoyld thee?

Lan. He that has spoyld himselfe, to make himselfe sport, and by his Coppie, will spoile all comes neere him, buy but a glasse, if you be yet so wealthy, and looke there who?

Val. Well said old Coppihold.

Lan. My hearts good freehold sir, and so youle finde it, this Gentleman your brother, your hopefull brother, for there is no hope of you, use him thereafter:

Val. Ene as well as I use my selfe, what wouldst thou have *Francke.*

Fran. Can you procure me a hundred pound:

Lan. Harke what he saies to you, O try your wits, they say you are excellent at it, for your land has laine long bed rid, and unsensible.

D   *Fran.*

Fran. And Ile forget all wrongs, you see my state, and to what wretchednesse, your will has brought me; but what it may be, by this benefit, if timely done, and like a noble brother, both you and I may feele, and to our comforts:

Val. (A hundred pound) dost thou know what thou hast said boy?

Fran. I said a hundred pound.

Val. Thou hast said more, then any man can justifie beleeve it, procure a hundred pounds, I say to thee, theres no such summe in nature, fortie shillings there may be now ith Mint, and thats a treasure, I have seene five pound, but let me tell it, and tis as wonderfull, as Calves with five legges, heeres five shillings *Francke*, the harvest of five weekes, and a good crop too, take it, and pay thy first fruites, Ile come downe and eate it out.

Fran. Tis patience must meete with you sir, not love.

Lan. Deale roundly, and leave these fiddle faddles:

Val. Leave thy prating, thou thinkest thou art a notable wise fellow, thou and thy rotten Sparrow hawke; two of the reverent.

Lan. I thinke you are mad, or if you be not will be, with the next moone, what would you have him doe.

Val. How?

Lan. To get money first, thats to live, you have shewed him how to want.

Val. Slife, how doe I live, why, what dull foole would aske that question, three hundred three pilds more, I and live bravely, the better halfe oth towne, and live most gloriously, aske them what states they have, or what annuities, or when they pray for seasonable harvests, thou hast a hansome wit, stirre into the world, *Francke*, stirre, stirre, for shame, thou art a pretty Scholler, aske how to live, write, write, write any thing, the worlds a fine beleeving world, write newes.

Lan. Dragons in *Sussex* sir, or fierie battles seene in the aire at *Aspurge*.

Val. Theres the way *Francke*, and in the taile of these, fright me the Kingdome with a sharpe Prognostication, that shal scowre them, dearth upon dearth, like leven taffaties, pre-
dictions

dictions of Sea breaches, warres, and want of herrings on our coast, with bloody noses.

Lan. Whirle windes, that shall take of the toppe of *Grantam* steeple, and clap it on *Poules*, and after these, a Lenvoy to the Citty for their sinnes.

Val. Probatum est, thou canst not want a pension, go switch me up a Covey of young Schollers, theres twenty nobles, and two loades of coales, are not these ready wayes. Cosmography thou art deepely read in, draw me a mappe from the Mermaide, I meane a midnight mappe to scape the watches, and such long sencelesse examinations, and Gentlemen shall feede thee, right good Gentlemen, I cannot stay long.

Lan. You have read learnedly, and would you have him follow these megeras, did you beginne with ballads.

Fran. Well, I will leave you, I see my wants are growne ridiculous, yours may be so, I will not curse you neither; you may thinke, when these wanton fits are over, who bred me, and who ruined me, looke to your selfe sir, a providence I waite on.

Val. Thou art passionate, hast thou beene brought up with girles.

Enter Shorthose with a bagge.

Short. Rest you merry Gentlemen.

Val. Not so merry as you suppose sir.

Short. Pray stay a while, and let mee take a view of you, I may put my spoone into the wrong pottage pot else.

Val. Why wilt thou muster us.

Short. No you are not he, you are a thought too hansome.

Lan. Who wouldst thou speake withall, why doest thou peepe so?

Short. I am looking birds nests, I can finde none in your bush beard, I would speake with you blacke Gentleman.

Fran. With me my friend.

Short. Yes sure, and the best friend sir, it seemes you spake withall this twelve moneths Gentleman, theres money for you.

Val. How?

Short. Theres none for you sir, be not so briefe, not a penny, law how he itches at it, stand of, you stirre my colour.

Lance. Take it, tis money.

Short. You are too quicke too, first be sure you have it, you seeme to be a Faulckoner, but a foolish one.

Lan. Take it, and say nothing:

Short. You are cosend too, tis take it, and spent it.

Fran. From whom came i, sir.

Short. Such another word, and you shall have none ont.

Fran. I thanke you sir, I doubly thanke you.

Short. Well sir, then buy you better clothes, and get your hat drest, and your Laundresse to wash your bootes white.

Fran. Pray stay sir, may you not be mistaken.

Short. I thinke I am, give me the money again, come quick, quicke, quicke.

Fran. I would be loath to render, till I am sure it be so.

Short. Harke in your eare, is not your name *Franscisco*.

Fran. Yes.

Short. Be quiet then, it may thunder a hundred times, before such stones fall; doe not you neede it.

Fran. Yes.

Short. And tis thought you have it.

Fran. I thinke I have.

Short. Then hold it fast, tis not flyblowne, you may pay for the poundage, you forget your selfe, I have not seene a Gentleman so backward, a wanting Gentleman.

Fran. Your mercy sir.

Short. Freind you have mercy, a whole bagge full of mercy, be merry with it, and be wise.

Fran. I would faine if it please you, but know.

Short. It does not please me, tell over your money and be not mad boy.

Val. You have no more such bagges:

Short. More such there are sir, but few I feare for you, I have cast your water, you have wit, you need no money. *Exit*

Lan. Be not amazed sir tis good gold, good old gold, this is restorative, and in good time, it comes to doe you good, keepe it and use it, let honest fingers feele it, yours be too quicke sir.

Fran. He named me, and he gave it me, but from whom.

Lance.

Lan. Let um send more, and then examine it, this can be but a preface.

Fran. Being a stranger, of whom can I deserve this.

Lan. Sir, if any man that has but eyes, and manly understanding to finde mens wants, good men are bound to doe so.

Val. Now you see *Francke*, there are more waies then certainties, now you beleeve: What plow brought you this harvest, what sale of timber, coales, or what annuities, these feede no hindes, nor waite the expectation of quarter dayes, you see it showers into you, you are an asse, lie plodding, and lie fooleing, about this blazing starre, and that bopeepe, whyneing, and fasting, to finde the naturall reason why a dogge turnes twice about before he lie downe, what use of these, or what joy in annuities, where every mans thy studdy, and thy tennant, I am ashamed on thee:

Lan. Yes I have seene this fellow, theres a wealthy Widdow hard by.   *Val.* Yes marry is there.

Lan. I thinke hees her servant, I am cosend if after her, I am sure ont.

Fran. I am glad ont.

Lan. Shees a good woman.

Fran. I am gladder:

Lan. And young enough beleeve.

Fran. I am gladder of all sir.

Val. Franck, you shall lye with me soone.

Fran. I thanke my money:

Lan. His money shall lie with mee, three in a bed sir will be too much this weather.   (things ——

Val. Meete me at the Mermaide, and thou shalt see what

Lan. Trust to your selfe sir.   *Exeunt Fran. and Vall.*

Enter Fount, Bella, and Vallentine.

Fount. O *Vallentine.*

Val. How now, why doe you looke so.

Bella. The Widdowes going man.

Val. Why let her goe man.

Hare. Shees going out oth Towne.

Val. The Townes the happier, I would they were all gone

Fount. We cannot come to speake with her.

Val. Not to speake to her.
Bel. She will be gone within this houre, either now *Valle*.
Fount. Hare. Now, now, now, good *Vall*.
Val. I had rather march ith mouth oth Cannon, but adiew, if she be above ground, goe, away to your praiers, away I say, away, she shall be spoken withall. *Exeunt*

Enter Shorthose with one boote on, Roger & Humphrey.

Rog. She will goe *Shorthose*.
Short. Who can helpe it *Roger*?
Within Raphe. *Roger* helpe downe with the hangings.
Rog. By and by *Raph*, I am making up oth trunckes here.
Raph. Shorthose.
Short. Well.
Raph. Who lookes to my Ladies Wardrobe? *Humphrey*.
Hum. Heere.
Raph. Downe with the boxes in the gallery, and bring away the Coach Cushions.
Short. Will it not raine, no conjuring abroad, nor no devises to stop this journey.
Rog. Why goe now, why now, why oth sudden, now what preparation, what horses have we ready, what provision laid in ith Country.
Hum. Not an egge I hope.
Rog. No nor one drop of good drink boyes, ther's the devil.
Short. I heartily pray the malt be musty, and then we must
Hum What saies the Steward? (come up againe.
Rog. Hees at's wits end, for some foure houres since, out of his haste and providence, he mistooke the Millers maunjey mare, for his owne nagge.
Short. And she may breake his necke, and save the journey, oh *London* how I love thee.
Hum. I have no bootes, nor none Ile buy (or if I had) refuse me if I would venture my abillity, before a cloake bagge, men are men.
Short. For my part, if I be brought, as I know it will be aimed at, to carry any durty dairy creame pot, or any gentle Lady of the Laundry, chambring, or wantonnesse behinde my gelding, with all her streamers, knapsackes, glasses, gu-
gawes,

gawes, as if I were a running flippery, Ile give um leave to cut my girts, and flay me. Ile not be troubled with their diftibations, at every halfe miles end, I underftand my felfe, and am refolved.

Hum. To morrow night at *Olivers*, who fhalbe there boyes, who fhall meete the wenches.

Rog. The well brued ftand of Ale, we fhould have met at.

Short. Thefe griefes like to another tale of *Troy*, would mollifie the hearts of barbarous people, and Tom Butcher weepe *Eneas enters*, and now the townes loft.

Ral. Why whether run you, my Lady is mad.

Short. I would fhe were in Bedlam.

Ral. The carts are come, no hands to helpe to load um, the ftuffe lies in the hall, the plate:

Within Widdow. Why knaves there, where be thefe idle fellowes

Short. Shall I ride with one boote.

Wid. Why where I fay:

Ral. Away, away, it muft be fo.

Short. O for a tickling ftorme, to laft but ten dayes. *Exeunt*

Actus 3. Scan. 1.

Enter Ifabella and Luce.

Luce. BY my troth Miftris I did it for the beft:

Ifa. It may be fo, but *Luce*, you have a tongue: a difh of meate in your mouth, which if it were minced *Luce*, would doe a great deale better.

Luc. I proteft Miftreffe.

Ifa. It will be your owne one time or other: *Walter.*

Walter within: Anon forfooth.

Ifa. Lay my hat ready, my fanne and cloake, you are fo full of providence; and *Walter*, tucke up my little box behinde the Coach, and bid my maide make ready, my fweete fervice to your good Lady Miftreffe; and my dog, good let the Coachman carry him.

Luc. But heare me.

Ifa. I am in love fweete *Luce*, and you are fo skillfull, that I muft must needes undoe my selfe; and heare me, let *Oliver* packe up my glasse discreetly, and see my Curles well carried, O sweete *Luce*, you have a tongue, and open tongues have open you know what *Luce*.

Luce. Pray you be satisfied.

Isa. Yes and contented too, before I leave you: theres a *Roger*, which some call a Butcher, I speake of certainties, I doe not fish *Luce*, nay doe not stare, I have a tongue can talke too; and a greene Chamber *Luce*, a backe doore opens to a long gallery; there was a night *Luce*, doe you perceive, doe you perceive me yet: O doe you blush *Luce*: a Friday night I saw your Saint *Luce*; for tother box of Marmaladde, alls thine sweete *Roger*, this I heard and kept too.

Luce. Ene as you are a woman Mistresse.

Isa. This I allow as good and physicall sometimes these meetings, and for the cheering of the heart; but *Luce*, to have your owne turne served, and to your friend to be a dogbolt.

Luce. I confesse it Mistresse.

Isa. As you have made my sister Iealous of me and foolishly, and childishly pursued it, I have found out your haunt, and traced your purposes, for which mine honour suffers, your best wayes must be applied to bring her backe againe, and seriously and suddenly, that so I may have a meanes to cleare my selfe, and she a faire opinion of me, else you peevish——

Luce. My power and prayers Mistresse.

Isa. Whats the matter.

Enter Shorthose and Widdow.

Short. I have beene with the Gentleman, he has it, much good may doe him with it.

Wid. Come are you ready, you love so to delay time, the day growes on.

Isa. I have sent for a few trifles, when those are come; And now I know your reason.

Wid. Know your owne honour then, about your businesse, see the Coach ready presently, Ile tell you more then;

Exit Luce and Shorthose.

And understand it well; you must not thinke my sister, so

tender

tender eyed as not to see your follies, alas I know your heart, and must imagine, and truely too; tis not your charitie can coyne such sums to give a way as you have done, in that you have no wisedome *Isabel*, no nor modestie where nobler uses are at home; I tell you, I am ashamed to finde this in your yeares, farre more in your discretion, none to chuse but things for pittie, none to seale your thoughts on, but one of no abiding, of no name; nothing to bring you but this, cold and hunger: A jolly Ioynture sister, you are happy, no mony, no not tenne shillings.

Isa. You search nearely.

Wid. I know it as I know your folly, one that know not where he shall eate his next meale, take his rest, unlesse it be in th stockes; what kindred has he, but a more wanting brother, or what vertues.

Isa. You have had rare intelligence, I see sister.

Wid. Or say the man had vertue, is vertue in this age a full inheritance: what Ioynture can he make you, *Plutarchs Moralls*, or so much peenny rent in the small pots, this is not well, tis weake, and I grive to know it.

Isa. And this you quit the towne for.

Wid. Its not time.

Isa. You are better read in my affaires than I am, thats all I have to answer, Ile goe with you, and willingly, and what you thinke most dangerous, Ile sit and laugh at.
For sister tis not folly but good discretion governes our maine Fortunes.

Wid. I am glad to heare you say so.

Isa. I am for you.

Enter Shorthose and Humphrey with riding rods.

Hum. The devill cannot stay her, she'le ont, eate an egge now, and then we must away.

Short. I am gaulled already, yet I will pray may London wayes from henceforth be full of holes, and Coaches cracke their wheeles, may zealous Smithes so housell all our Hackneyes, that they may feele compunction in their feete, and tire at Highgate, may it raine above all Almanackes till carriers saile, and the Kings Fishmonger ride like *Bike Arion* up-

Wit without Money

on a Trout to London.

Hum. At S. *Albones*, let all the Innes be drunke, not an Host sober to bid her worship welcome.

Short. Not a Fiddle, but all preacht downe with Puritans; no meate but legges of beefe.

Hum. No beds but Woollpackes.

Short. And those so crammed with warrens of sterved Fleas that bite like bandogges; let *Mims* be angry at their S. Bellswagger, and we passe in the heate ont and be beaten, beaten abominably, beaten horse and man, and all my Ladies linnen sprinkled with suddes and dishwater.

Short. Not a wheele but out of joynt.

Enter Roger laughing.

Hum. Why dost thou laugh.

Rog. Theres a Gentleman, and the rarest Gentleman, and makes the rarest sport. *Short.* Where, where?

Rog. Within here, has made the gayest sport with *Tim* the Coachman, so tewed him up with sacke that hee lies lashing a butt of Malmsie for his Mares.

Short. Tis very good.

Rog. And talkes and laughes, and singes the rarest songs, and *Shorthose*, he has so mauld the red Deere pies, made such an almes ith butterie.

Short. Better still. *Enter Vall. Widdow.*

Hum. My Lady in a rage with the Gentleman.

Short. May he anger her into a feather. *Exeunt.*

Wid. I pray tell me, who sent you hether? for I imagine it is not your condition you looke so temperately, and like a Gentleman, to aske me these milde questions.

Val. Doe you thinke I use to walke of errands gentle Lady, or deale with women out of dreames from others.

Wid. You have not knowne me sure?

Val. Not much.

Wid. What reason have you then to be so tender of my credit, you are no kinsman.

Val. If you take it so, the honest office that I came to doe you, is not so heavy but I can returne it: now I perceive you are too proud, not worth my visit.

Wid.

Wid. Pray stay, alittle sproud.

Val. Monstrous proud, I grieve to heare a woman of your value, and your abundant parts stung by the people, but now I see tis true, you looke upon mee as if I were a rude and sawcie fellow that borrowed all my breeding from a dunghill, or such a one, as should now fall and worship you in hope of pardon: you are cosen'd Lady, I came to prove opinion a loud lier, to see a woman onely great in goodnesse, and Mistresse of a greater fame than fortune, but—

Wid. You are a strange Gentleman, if I were proud now, I should be monstrous angry, which J am not, and shew the effects of pride; I should dispise you, but you are welcome sir: To thinke well of our selves, if we deserve it, is a luster in us, and every good we have; strives to show gracious, what use is it else, old age like Seer trees, is seldome seene affected, stirs sometimes at rehearsall of such acts his daring youth endeavour'd.

Val. This is well, and now you speake to the purpose, you please me, but to be place proud:

Wid. If it be our owne, why are we set here with distinction else, degrees, and orders given us, in you men, tis held a coolenesse if you lose your right afronts, and losse of honour: streetes, and walls, and upper ends of tables, had they tongues could tell what blood has followed, and what sude about your rankes; are we so much below you, that till you have us, are the toppes of nature, to be accounted drones, without a difference, you will make us beasts indeed.

Val. Nay worse then this too, proud of your cloathes, they sweare a Mercers Lucifer, a tumer tackt together by a Taylor, nay yet worse, proud of red and white, a varnish that buttermilke can better.

Wid. Lord how little will vex these poore blinde people, if my cloathes be sometimes gay and glorious, does it follow my minde must be my Mercers too, or say my beauty please some weake eyes, must it pleale them to thinke that blowes mee up, that every houre blowes of: this is an Infants anger.

Val. Thus they say too, what though you have a Coach lined

lined through with velvet and foure faire Flaunders Mares, why should the streets be troubled continually with you, till Carmen curse you, can there be ought in this but pride of shew Lady, and pride of bum-beating, till the learned lawyers with their fat bagges, are thrust against the bulkes till all their Cases cracke; why should this Lady, and tother Lady, and the third sweete Ladie, and Madam at mile end, be dailie visited, and your poorer neighbours, with course napses neglected, fashions confer'd about, pouncings, and paintings, and young mens bodies read on like Anotamies.

Wid. You are very credulous, and somewhat desperate to deliver this sir, to her you know not, but you shall confesse me, and finde I will not start; in us all meetings lie open to these leud reports, and our thoughts at Church, our very meditations some will sweare, which all should feare to judge, at least uncharitably, are mingled with your memories, cannot sleepe, but this sweet Gentleman swimmes in our fancies, that scarlet man of warre, and that smooth Senior; not dresse our heads without new ambushes how to surprise that greatnesse or that glory; our very smiles are subject to constructions; nay sir, its come to this, we cannot pish, but tis a favour for some foole or other: should we examine you thus, wert not possible to take you without Prospectives.

Val. It may be, but these excuse not.

Wid. Nor yours force no truth sir, what deadly tongues you have, and to those tongues what hearts, and what inventions; ah my conscience, and 'twere not for sharpe justice, you would venture to aime at your owne mothers, and account it glory to say you had done so; all you thinke are Counsells and cannot erre, tis we still that shew double, giddie, or gorg'd with passion; we that build Babells for mens confusions, we that scatter as day do's his warme light; our killing curses over Gods creatures next to the devills mallice: lets intreate your good words.

Val. Well, this woman has a brave soule.

Wid. Are not we gaily blest then, and much beholding to you for your substance; you may doe what you list, we what beseemes us, and narrowly doe that too, and precisely, our

names

Wit without Money.

names are served in else at Ordinaries, and belcht a broad in Tavernes.

Val. O most brave Wench, and able to redeeme an age of women.

Wid. You are no Whoremasters, alas no Gentlemen, it were an impudencie to thinke you vicious; you are so holy, handsome Ladies fright you, you are the coole things of the time, the temperance, meere emblems of the Law, and vales of Vertue, you are not daily mending like Dutch Watches, & plastering like old walls; they are not Gentlemen, that with their secret sinnes encrease our Surgeons, and lie in forraine Countries, for new sores; women are all these vices; you are not envious, false, covetous, vaineglorious, irreligious, drunken, revengefull, giddie-eyed, like Parrats, eaters of others honours.

Val. You are angry.

Wid. No by my troth, and yet I could say more too, for when men make me angry, I am miserable.

Val. Sure tis a man she could not beare it thus bravely else, it may be I am tedious.

Wid. Not at all sir, I am content at this time you should trouble me.

Val. You are distrustfull.

Wid. Where I finde no truth sir.

Val. Come, come you are full of passion.

Wid. Some I have, I were too neere the nature a god else.

Val. You are monstrous peevish.

Wid. Because they are monstrous foolish, and know not how to use that should trie me.

Val. I was never answered thus, was you never drunke Lady?

Wid. No sure, not drunke sir? yet I love good wine as I love health and joy of heart, but temperately, why doe you aske that question?

Val. For that sinne that they most charge you with, is this sinnes servant, they say you are monstrous.

Wid. What sir, what?

Val. Most strangely.

Wid. It has a name sure.

Val. Infinitly lustfull, without all bounds, they sweare you kild your husband.

Wid. Lets have it all for heavens sake, tis good mirth sir.

Val. They say you will have foure now, and those foure stucke in foure quarters like foure windes to coole you; will she not cry nor curse?

Wid. On with your Story.

Val. And that you are forcing out of dispensations with summes of money to that purpose.

Wid. Foure husbands, should not I be blest sir; for example, Lord what should I doe with them, turne a Malt mill, or tyth them out like towne Bulls to my tennants, you come to make me angry, but you cannot.

Val. Ile make you merry then, you are a brave woman, and in dispite of envie a right one, goe thy wayes, truth thou art as good a woman, as any Lord of them all can lay his legge over, I doe not often commend your sexe.

Wid. It seemes so, your commendations are so studied for.

Val. I came to see you, and sift you into flower, to know your purenesse, and I have found you excellent I thanke you; continue so, and shew men how to tread, and women how to follow : get an husband, an honest man, you are a good woman, and live hedg'd in from scandall, let him be too an understanding man, and to that steedfast; tis pittie your faire Figure should miscarrie, and then you are fixt, farewell.

Wid. Pray stay a little, I love your company now you are so pleasant, and to my disposition set so even.

Va. I can no longer. *Exit.*

Wid. As I live a fine fellow, this manly handsome bluntnesse, shewes him honest; what is he, or from whence? blesse me, foure husbands, how prettily he fooled me into vices, to stirre my jealousie and finde my nature, a proper Gentleman, I am not well oth' sudden, such a companion I could live and die with, his angers are meere mirth. *Enter Isabella.*

Isa. Come, come, I am ready.

Wit Are you so?

Isa. What ailes she, the Coach staies, and the people, the
day

Wit without Money.

day goes on, I am as ready now as you desire sister: fie, who stayes now, why doe you sit and pout thus.

Wid. Prethee be quiet, I am not well.

Isab. For heavens sake lets not ride staggering in the night, come, pray you take some sweete meates in your pocket, if your stomacke ——

Wid. I have a little businesse.

Isa. To abuse me, you shall not finde new dreames, and new suspitions, to horse withall.

Wid. Lord who made you a Commander: hay ho, my heart. *Isa.* Is the winde come thether, and coward like doe you lose your colours to um, are you sicke ath *Velentine*; sweete sister, come lets away, the countrey will so quicken you, and we shall live so sweetely: *Luce*, my Ladies cloake; nay, you have put me into such a gogge of going I would not stay for all the world; if I live here, you have so knocked this love into my head, that I shall love any body, and I finde my body, I know not how, so apt; pray lets be gone sister, I stand on thornes.

Wid. I prethee *Isabella*, I faith I have some businesse that concernes me, I will suspect no more, here, weare that for me, and Ile pay the hundred pound you owe your tayler.

Enter Shorthose 1. Roger, Humphrey, Ralph.

Isa. I had rather goe, but ——

Wid. Come walke within me, weele goe to Cardes, unsadle the horses.

Short. A Iubile, a Iubile, we stay boyes. *Exeunt.*

Enter Vncle, Lance, Fountaine, Bellamore, Harebraine following.

Unc. Are they behinde us.

Lance. Close, close, speake aloud sir.

Vnc. I am glad my nephew has so much discretion at length to finde his wants: did she entertaine him.

Lance. Most bravely, nobly, and gave him such a welcome.

Vnc. For his owne sake doe you thinke.

Lance. Most certaine sir, and in his owne cause bestir'd himselfe too, and wan such liking from her, she dotes on him, has the command of all the house already.

Vnc. He deales not well with his friends.

Lance.

Lance. Let him deale on, and be his owne friend, hee has most neede of her. *Vnc.* I wonder they would put him.

Lance. You are in the right ont, a man that must raise himselfe, I knew he would cosen um, and glad I am he has, he watched occasion, and found it ith' nicke.

Vnc. He has deceived me.

Lance. I told you howsoever he weel'd about, hee would charge whom at length, how I could laugh now, to thinke of these tame fooles.

Vnc. Twas not well done, because they trusted him, yet.

Bel. Harke you Gentlemen.

Vnc. We are upon a businesse, pray excuse us, they have it home.   *Lanc.* Come let it worke good on Gentlemen.

Exit Vncle, Lance.

Fount. Tis true, he is a knave, I ever thought it.

Hare. And we are fooles, tame fooles.

Bel. Come lets goe seeke him, he shall be hang'd before he colt us basely.   *Exit.*   *Enter Isabella, Luce.*

Isa. Art sure she loves him.

Luce. Am I sure I live? And I have clap on such a commendation on your revenge.

Isa. Faith, he is a pretty Gentleman.

Luce. Handsome enough, and that her eye has found out.

Isa. He talkes the best they say, and yet the maddest.

Luce. Has the right way.   *Isa.* How is she?

Luce. Beares it well, as if she cared not, but a man may see with halfe an eye through all her forced behaviours, and finde who is her *Vallantine*.

Isa. Come lets goe see her, I long to prosecute.

Luce. By no meanes Mistresse, let her take better hold first.

Isa. I could burst now.   *Exeunt.*

Enter Vallentine, Fountaine, Bellamore, Harebraine.

Vall. Vpbraide me with your benefits, you Pilchers, you shotten, sold, slight fellowes, wast not I that undertooke you first from emptie barrells, and brought those barking mouthes that gaped like bung-holes to utter sence: where got you understanding? who taught you manners and apt carriage

Wit without Money.

carriage to ranke your selves? who filed you in fit Tavernes, were those borne with your worships when you came hether? what brought you from the Vniversities of moment matter to allow you, besides your small bare sentences?

Bell. Tis well sir.

Val. Long cloakes with two hand-rapiers, boot-hose with penny-poses, and twentie fooles opinions, who looked on you but piping rites that knew you would be prising, and Prentises in *Paules* Church-yard, that sented your want of *Brittanes* Bookes. *Enter Widdow, Luce, Harebraine.*

Fount. This cannot save you.

Val. Taunt my integretie you whelpes.

Bell. You may talke the stocke wee gave you out, but see no further.

Hare. You tempt our patience, we have found you out, and what your trust comes to, yeare well feathered, thanke us, and thinke now of an honest course, tis time; men now begin to looke, and narrowly into your tumbling trickes, they are stale.

Wid. Is not that he? *Luce.* Tis he.

Wid. Be still and marke him.

Val. How miserable will these poore wretches be when I forsake um, but things have their necessities, I am sorry, to what a vomit must they turne againe now to their owne deare dunghill breeding; never hope after I cast you off, you men of Motley, you most undone things below pittie, any that has a soule and sixe pence dares releeve you, my name shall barre that blessing; theres your cloake sir, keepe it close to you, it may yet preserve you a fortnight longer from the foole; your hat, pray be covered, and theres the satt'n that your worships sent me, will serve you at a sizer yet.

Fount. Nay faith sir, you may ene rubbe these out now.

Val. No such relicke, nor the least ragge of such a sorded weakenesse shall keepe me warme, these breeches are mine owne, purchased, and paid for, without your compassion, and Christian bleeches founded in *Blacke Friers*, and so Ile maintaine um. *Hare.* So they seeme sir.

Val. Onely the thirteene shillings in these breeches, and the odde groat, I take it, shall be yours sir, a marke to know a knave by, pray preserve it, doe not displease me more, but

F   take

Wit without Money.

take it presently, now helpe me off with my bootes.

Hare. We are no groomes sir.

Val. For once you shall be, doe it willingly, or by this hand Ile make you.

Bell. To our owne sir, we may apply our hands.

Val. Theres your hangers, you may deserve a strong paire, and a girdle will hold you without buckles; now I am perfect, and now the proudest of your worships tell me I am beholding to you. *Fount.* No such matter.

Val. And take heede how you pitty me, tis dangerous, exceeding dangerous, to prate of pittie which are the poorer; you are now puppies; I without you, or you without my knowledge be rogues, and so be gone, be rogues and reply not, for if you doe ———

Bell. Onely thus much, and then weele leave you, the ayre is farre sharper than our anger sir, and these you may reserve to raile in warmer.

Hare. Pray have a care sir of your health. *Exit Lovers.*

Val. Yes hoghounds, more than you can have of your wits; tis cold, and I am very sensible, extreamely cold too, yet I will not off, till I have shamed these rascalls; I have endured as ill heates as another, and every way if one could perish my body, you'le beare the blame on't; I am colder here, not a poore penny left. *Vncle with a bagge.*

Vnc. Tas taken rarely, and now hees flead he will be ruled.

Lance. Too him, tew him, abuse him, and nip him close.

Vnc. Why how now cosen, sunning your selfe this weather?

Val. As you see sir, in a hot fit, I thanke my friends.

Vnc. But cosen, where are your cloathes man, those are no inheritance, your scruple may compound with those I take it, this is no fashion cosen.

Val. Not much followed, I must confesse; yet Vncle I determine to trie what may be done next Tearme.

Lance. How came you thus sir, for you are strangely moved.

Val. Ragges, toyes and trifles, fit onely for those fooles that first possessed um, and to those Knaves, they are rendred freemen Vncle; ought to appeare like innocents, old *Adam,* a faire Figge-leafe sufficient.

Vncle. Take me with you, were these your friends, that
clear'd

Wit without Money.

clear'd you thus.

Val. Hang friends, and even recknings that make friends.

Unc. I thought till now, there had beene no such living, no such purchase, for all the rest is labour, as a list of honourable friends, doe not such men as you sir, in liew of all your understandings, travells, and those great gifts of nature; aime at no more than casting off your coates, I am strangely cosend.

Lance. Should not the towne shake at the cold you feele now, and all the Gentry suffer intrediction, no more sence spoken, all things *Goth* and *Vandall*, till you be summed againe, velvets and scarlets, annointed with gold-lace, and cloth of silver turned into *Spanish* Cottens for a pennance, wits blasted with your bulls, and Tavernes withered, as though the tearme lay at S. *Albones*.

Val. Gentlemen you have spoken long, and levill, I beseech you take breath a while and here me; you imagine now, by the twirling of your strings, that I am at the last, as also that my friends are flowne like Swallowes after Summer.   *Unc.* Yes sir.

Val. And that I have no more in this poore pannier, to raise me up againe above your rents Vncle.

Unc. All this I doe beleeve.

Val. You have no minde to better me.

Unc. Yes cosen, and to that end I come, and once more offer you all that my power is master off.

Val. A match then, lay me downe fiftie pound there.

Unc. There it is sir.

Val. And on it write, that you are pleased to give this, as due unto my merit, without caution of land redeeming, tedious thankes, or thrift hereafter to be hoped for.

Unc. How?   *Luce layes a suite and letter at the doore.*

Val. Without dareing, when you are drunke, to rellish of revilings, to which you are prone in sacke Vncle.

Unc. I thanke you sir.

Lance. Come, come away, let the young wanton play a while, away I say sir, let him goe forward with his naked fashion, he will seeke you to morrow; goodly weather, sultrie hot, sultry, how I sweate.

Uncl. Farewell sir.

Wit without Money.

Vnc. Farewell sir. *Exeunt Vncle and Lance.*

Val. Would I sweat too, I am monstrous vext, and cold too; and these are but thinne pumpes to walke the steetes in; cloathes I must get, this fashion will not fadge with me, besides, tis an ill Winter weare, ----- What art thou? yes, they are cloathes, and rich ones, some foole has left um: and if I should utter ----- whats this paper here; let these be only worne, by the most noble and deserving Gentleman *Vallentine*, ---- dropt out oth' cloudes; I thinke they are full of gold too; well Ile leave my wonder, and be warme agen, in the next house Ile shift. *Exit.*

Actus 4. Scæna 1.

Enter Franscisco, Vncle, and Lance.

Fran. WHy doe you deale thus with him tis unnobly.
Vnc. Peace cosen peace, you are to tender of him, he must be dealt thus with, he must be cured thus, the violence of his disease *Francisco*, must not be jested with, tis growne infectious, and now strong corasives most cure him.

Lance. Has had a stinger, has eaten off his Cloathes, the next his skinne comes.

Vnc. And let it search him to the bones, tis better, twill make him feele it.

Lance. Where be his noble friends now? will his fantasticall opinions cloath him, or the learned Art of having nothing feede him.

Vnc. It must needes greedely, for all his friends have flung him off, he is naked, and where to skinne himselfe agen, if I know, or can devise how he should get himselfe lodging, his spirit must be bowed, and now we have him, have him at that we hoped for.

Lance. Next time we meete him cracking of Nuts, with halfe a clocke about him, for all meanes are cut off, or borrowing sixe pence, to shew his bountie in the pottage Ordinary. *Fran.* Which way went he?

Lance. Pox, Why should you aske after him, you have beene trim'd already, let him take his fortune, he spunne it out himselfe, sir, theres no pitty.

Vnc. Besides some good to you now, from this miserie.

Fran. I rise upon his ruines, fie, fie, Vncle, fie honest *Lance*, those Gentlemen were base people, that could so soone take fire to his destruction.

Vnc. You are a foole, you are a foole, a young man.

Enter Vallentine.

Val. Morrow Vncle, morrow *Francke*, sweete *Francke*, and how, and how dee, thinke now, how show matters; morrow Bandogge.   *Vnc.* How?

Fran. Is this man naked, forsaken of his friends.

Val. That't hansome *Francke*, a pretty Gentleman, ifaith thou lookest well, and yet here may be those that looke as hansome.

Lan. Sure he can conjure, and has the devill for his taylor.

Vnc. New and rich, tis most impossible he should recover.

Lan. Give him this lucke, and fling him into the Sea.

Vnc. Tis not he, imagination cannot worke this miracle.

Val. Yes, yes, tis he, I will assure you Vncle, the very he, the he your wisdome plaid withall, I thanke you fort, neyed at his nakednes, and made his cold and poverty, your pastime; you see I live, and the best can doe no more Vncle, and though I have no state, I keepe the streetes still; and take my pleasure in the towne, like a poore Gentleman, weare clothes to keepe me warme, poore things they serve me, can make a show too if I list, yes Vncle, and ring a peale in my pockets, ding dong, Vncle, these are mad foolish wayes, but who can helpe um.   *Vnc.* I am amazed.

Lan. Ile sell my coppyhold, for since there are such excellent new nothings, why should I labour, is there no fairy haunts him, no rat, nor no old woman.   *Vnc.* You are *Vallentine*.

Val. I thinke so, I cannot tell, I have beene cald so, and some say christened, why doe you wonder at me, and swell, as if you had met a sarjeant fasting, did you ever know desert want, yare fooles, a little stoope, there may be to allay him, he would grow too ranke else, a small eclipse, to shaddow him, but out hee must breake, glowingly againe, and with a great luster, looke you Vncle, motion, and Majesty.

Vnc. I am confounded.   *Fran.* I am of his faith.

F 3   *Val.*

Val. Walke by his carelesse kinsman, and turne againe and walke, and looke thus Vncle, taking some one by the hand, he loves best, leave them to the mercy of the hog market, come *Franke,* Fortune is now my friend, let me instruct thee.

Fran. Good morrow Vncle, I must needes goe with him.

Val. Flay me, and turne me out where none inhabits, within two houres, I shall be thus againe, now wonder on, and laugh at your owne ignorance. *Ex. Vall. & Franck.*

Unc. I doe beleeve him.

Lan. So doe I, and heartily upon my conscience bury him starke naked, he would rise againe, within two houres imbroidered: sow musterd seedes, and they cannot come up so thicke as his new sattens doe, and clothes of silver, theres no striving. *Unc.* Let him play a while then, and lets search out what band:

Lan. I there the game lyes. *Exeunt*

Enter Fountaine, Bellamore and Harebraine.

Foun. Come lets speake for our selves, we have lodg'd him sure enough, his nakednesse dare not peepe out to crosse us.

Bel. We can have no admittance.

Hare. Lets in boldly, and use our best arts, who she daines to favour, we are all content.

Foun. Much good may doe her with him, no civill warres.

Bel. By no meanes, now doe I wonder in what old tod Ivy hee lies whistling for meanes, nor clothes hee has none, nor none will trust him, we have made that side sure, teach him a new wooing. *Hare.* Say it is his Vncles spite.

Foun. It is all one Gentlemen, 'tas rid us of a faire incumbrance, and makes us looke about to our owne fortunes. Who are these. *Enter Isabell and Luce.*

Isa. Not see this man yet, well, I shall be wiser: but *Luce* didst ever know a woman melt so, she is finely hurt to hunt.

Luc. Peace, the three suitors.

Isa. I could so titter now and laugh, I was lost *Luce,* and I must love, I know not what; O *Cupid,* what pretty gins thou hast to halter woodcockes, and we must into the Countrey in all hast *Luce.* *Luce.* For heavens sake Mistris.

Isa. Nay I have done, I must laugh though, but scholler, I shall teach you. *Foun.* Tis her sister.

Bel.

Wit without Money.

Bell. Save you Ladies. *Isa.* Faire met Gentlemen, you are visiting my sister, I assure my selfe.

Hart. We would faine blesse our eyes.

Isa. Behold and welcome, you would see her:

Foun. Tis our businesse.

Isa. You shall see her, and you shall talke with her.

Luce. Shee will not see um, not spend a word.

Isa. Ile make her fret a thousand, nay now I have found the scab, I will so scratch her. *Luc.* She cannot endure um.

Isa. She loves um but too dearely, come follow me, Ile bring you toth party Gentlemen, then make your owne conditions.

Luc. She is sicke you know.

Isa. Ile make her well, or kill her, and take no idle answer, you are fooles then, nor stand off for her state, sheele scorne you all then, but urge her still, and though she fret, still follow her, a widdow must be wonne so.

Bel. Shee speakes bravely.

Isa. I would faine have a brother in law, I love mens company, and if she call for dinner to avoide you, be sure you stay, follow her into her chamber, if she retire to pray, pray with her, and boldly, like honest lovers.

Luc. This will kill her.

Foun. You have showed us one way, do but lend the tother.

Isa. I know you stand a thornes, come Ile dispatch you.

Luc. If you live after this. *Isa.* I have lost my ayme.

Enter Vallentine and Franscisco.

Fra. Did you not see um since.

Val. No hang um, hang um.

Fra. Nor will you not be seene by um: *Val.* Let um alone *Francke*, Ile make um their owne justice, and a jerker.

Fra. Such base discurteous dogge whelpes.

Val. I shall dogge um, and double dog um, ere I have done.

Fran. Will you goe with me, for I would faine finde out this peece of bountie, it was the widdows man, that I am certaine of. *Val.* To what end would you goe.

Fran. To give thankes sir.

Val. Hang giving thankes, hast not thou parts deserves it, it includes to a further will to be beholding, beggers can doe no more at doores, if you will goe there lies your way.

Fran.

Fran. I hope you will goe.

Val. No not in ceremony, and to a woman, with mine owne father, were hee living *Francke*, I would toth Court with beares first, if it be that wench, I thinke it is, for tothers wiser, I would not be so lookt upon, and laught at, so made a ladder for her wit, to climbe upon, for tis the rarest ti in Christendome, I know her well *Francke*, and have buckled with her, so lickt, and stroakt, fleard upon, and flouted, and showne to Chambermaides, like a strange beast, she had purchased with her penny. (woman

Fran. You are a strange man, but doe you thinke it was a

Val. Theres no doubt ont, who can be there to doe it else, besides the manner of the circumstances.

Fran. Then such courtesies, who ever does um sir, saving your owne wisdome, must be more lookt into, and better answerd, then with deserving slights, or what we ought to have conferd upon us, men may starve else, meanes are not gotton now, with crying out I am a gallant fellow, a good souldier, a man of learning, or fit to be employed, immediate blessings, cease like miracles, and we must grow, by second meanes, I pray goe with me, even as you love me sir.

Val. I will come to thee, but *Francke*, I will not stay to heare your fopperies, dispatch those ere I come.

Fran. You will not faile me.

Val. Some two houres hence expect me.

Fran. I thanke you, and will looke for you. *Exeunt*

Enter Widdow, Shorthose, and Roger.

Wid. Who let me in these puppies, you blinde rascals, you drunken knaves severall.

Short. Yes forsooth, Ile let um in presently,--- gentlemen,

Wid. Spercious you blowne pudding, you bawling rogue.

Short. I bawle as loud as I can, would you have me fetch um upon my backe. *Wid.* Get um out rascall, out with um, out, I sweate to have um neare me.

Short. I should sweate more to carry um out.

Rog. They are Gentlemen Madam:

Shor. Shall we get um intoth butterie, and make um drinke.

Wid. Doe any thing, so I be eased.

Enter

Wit without Money.

Enter Isabel, Fount, Bella, Hare.

Isa. Now too her sir, feare nothing.

Rog. Slip a side boy, I know shee loves um, howsoere shee carries it, and has invited um, my young Mistris told me so.

Short. Away to tables then. *Exeunt.*

Isa. I shall burst with the sport one.

Fount. You are too curious Madam, too full of preparation, we expect it not.

Bella. Methinkes the house is hansome, every place decent, what neede you be so vext.

Hare. We are no strangers.

Foun. What though we come ere you expected us, doe not we know your entertainements Madam are free, and full at all times. *Wid.* You are merry Gentlemen.

Ball. We come to be merry Madam, and very merry, me live to laugh heartily, and now and then Lady a little of our old plea.

Wid. I am busie, and very busie too, will none deliver me.

Hare. There is a time for all, you may be busie, but when your friends come, you have as much power Madam.

Wid. This is a tedious torment.

Foun. How hansomely this title peece of anger shewes upon her, well Madam well, you know not how to grace your selfe.

Bella. Nay every thing she does breedes a new sweetnesse.

Wid. I must goe up, I must goe up, I have a businesse waites upon me, some wine for the Gentlemen.

Hare. Nay, weele goe with you, we never saw your chambers yet. *Isa.* Hold there boyes.

Wid. Say I goe to my prayers.

Foun. Weele pray with you, and helpe your meditations.

Wid. This is boystrous, or say I goe to sleepe, will you goe te sleepe with me.

Bel. So suddenly before meate will bee dangerous, wee know your dinners ready Lady, you will not sleepe.

Wid. Give me my Coach, I will take the aire,

Hare. Weele waite on you, and then your meate after a quickned stomacke.

Wid. Let it alone, and call my steward to mee, and bid him bring

Wit without Money.

bring his recknings into the Orchard, these unmannerly rude
puppies —— *Exit Widdow.*

Foun. Weeld walke after you and view the pleasure of the
place. *Isa.* Let her not rest, for if you give her
breath, sheele scorne and floute you, seeme how she will, this
is the way to winne her, be bold and prosper.

Bella. Nay if we doe not tire her. —— *Exeunt.*

Isa. Ile teach you to worme me good Lady sister, and peepe
into my privacies to suspect me, Ile torture you, with that you
hate most daintily, and when I have done that, laugh at that
you love most. *Enter Luce.*

Luc. What have you done, shee chafes and fumes outragi-
ously, and still they persecute her.

Isa. Long may they doe so, Ile teach her to declaime against
my pitties, why is shee not gone out oth' towne, but gives
occasion for men to run mad after her.

Luc. I shall be hanged.

Isa. This in me had beene high treason, three at a time, and
private in her Orchard, I hope sheele cast her reckonings
right now. *Enter Widdow.*

Wid. Well, I shall finde who brought um.

Isa. Ha, ha, ha.

Wid. Why doe you laugh sister, I feare me tis your tricke,
twas neatly done of you, and well becomes your pleasure.

Isa. What have you done with um.

Wid. Lockt um ith Orchard, there Ile make um dance and
caper too, before they get their liberty, unmannerly rude puppies.

Isa. They are somewhat saucy, but yet Ile let um out, and
once more hound um, why were they not beaten out.

Wid. I was about it, but because they came as suiters.

Isa. Why did you not answer um.

Wid. They are so impudent they will receive none: More
yet, how came these in.
Enter Franscisco and Lance.

Lan. At the doore Madam.

Isa. It is that face.

Luc. This is the Gentleman.

Wid. Shee sent the money too.

Wit without Money.

Luc. The same.

Isa. Ile leave you, they have some businesse.

Wid. Nay you shall stay sister, they are strangers both to me: how her face alters.

Isa. I am sorry he comes now.

Wid. I am glad he is here now though, who would you speake with Gentlemen? *Lan.* You Lady, or your faire sister there, heres a Gentleman, that has received a benefit.

Wid. From whom sir.

Lan. From one of you, as he supposes Madam, your man delivered it. *Wid.* I pray goe forward.

Lan. And of so great a goodnesse, that he dares not, without the tender of his thankes and service, passe by the house.

Wid. Which is the Gentleman?

Lan. This Madam.

Wid. Whats your name Sir?

Fran. They that know me call me *Franscisco* Lady, one not so proud to scorne, so timely a benefit, nor so wretched, to hide a gratitude.

Wid. It is well bestowed then.

Fran. Your faire selfe, or your sister as it seemes, for what desert I dare not know, unlesse a hansome subject for your charities, or aptnesse in your noble wils to doe it, have showred upon my wants, a timely bounty, which makes me rich in thankes, my best inheritance.

Wid. I am sorry twas not mine, this is the Gentlewoman, sie doe not blush goe roundly to the matter, the man is a prettie man. *Isa.* You have three fine ones.

Fran. Then to you deare Lady.

Isa. I pray no more Sir, if I may perswade you, your onely aptnesse to doe this is recompence, and more then I expected.

Fran. But good Lady.

Isa. And for me further to be acquainted with it, besides the imputation of vaine glory, were greedie thankings of my selfe, I did it not to be more affected to; I did it, and if it happened where I thought it fitted, I have my end, more to enquire is curious in either of us, more then that sulpicious:

Fran. But gentle Ladie, twill be necessary.

Isa. About the right way nothing, doe not fright it, being to pious use and tender sighted, with the blown face of complements, it blasts it had you not come at all, but thought thankes; it had beene too much, twas not to see your person.

Wid. A brave dissembling rogue, and how she carries it.

Isa. Though I beleeve few handsomer; or heare you, though I affect a good tongue well; or try you, though my yeares desire a friend, that I relieved you.

Wid. A plaguie cunning queane.

Isa. For so I carryed it, my ends too glorious in mine eies, and bartred the goodnesse I propounded with opinion.

Wid. Feare her not Sir.

Isa. You cannot catch me sister.

Fran. Will you both teach, and tie my tongue up Lady?

Isa. Let it suffice you have it, it was never mine, whilst good men wanted it.

Lan. This is a Saint sure.

Isa. And if you be not such a one restore it.

Fran. To commend my selfe were more officious, then you thinke my thankes are, to doubt I may be worth your gift a treason, both to mine owne good, and understanding, I know my mind cleare, and though modesty tels me, he that intreates intrudes, yet I must thinke something, and of some season, met with your better taste, this had not beene else.

Wid. What ward for that Wench.

Isa. Alas it never touched me.

Fran. Well gentle Ladie, yours is the first money I ever tooke upon a forced ill manners.

Isa. The last of me, if ever you use other.

Fran. How may I doe, and your way to be thought a gratefull taker. *Isa.* Spend it and say nothing, your modestie may deserve more.

Wid. O sister, will you barre thankefullnesse?

Isa. Dogges dance for meate, would you have men doe worse, for they can speake, cry out like Woodmongers, good deeds by the hundreds, I did it that my best friend should not know it, wine and vaine glory does as much as I else, if you will force my merit, against my meaning, use it in well bestowing it, in showing it came to be a benefit, and was so; and not examining a woman did it, or to what end, in not be-

leeving

leeving sometimes your selfe, when drinke and stirring conversation may ripen strange perswasions.

Fran. Gentle Lady, J were a base receiver of a curtesie, and you a worse disposer, were my nature unfurnished of these foresights, Ladies honours were ever in my thoughts, unspotted crimes, their good deedes holy temples, where the incense burnes not, to common eyes your feares are vertuous, and so I shall preserve um.

Isa. Keepe but this way, and from this place to tell me so, you have paid me; and so J wish you see all fortune. *Ex.*

Wid. feare not the woman will be thanked, I doe not doubt it, are you so crafty, carry it so precisely, this is to wake my feares, or to abuse mee, I shall looke narrowly, despaire not Gentlemen, there is an houre to catch a woman in, if you be wise, so, I must leave you too; now will I goe laugh at my suitors.   *Exit*

Lan. Sir what courage.

Fran. This woman is a founder, and scites statutes to all her benefits.

Lan. I never knew yet, so few yeares and so cunning, yet beleeve me she has an itch, but how to make her confesse it, for it is a crafty tit, and playes about you, will not bite home, she would faine, but she dares not; carry your selfe but so discreetely Sir, that want or wantonnesse seeme not to search you, and you shall see her open.

Fran. I do love her, and were I rich, would give two thousand pound to wed her wit but one houre, oh tis a dragon, and such a spritely way of pleasure, ha *Lance*.

Lan. Your ha *Lance* broken once, you would cry, ho, ho, *Lance*.

Fran. Some leaden landed rogue, will have this Wench now, when alls done, some such youth will carry her, and weare her greasie out like stuffe, some dunce that knowes no more but Markets, and admires nothing but a long charge at files: O the fortunes.

Enter Isabel and Luce.

Lan. Comfort your selfe.

Luc. They are here yet, and a love too, boldly upont, Nay Mistresse, I still told you, how 'would finde your trust, this

Wit without Money.

tis to venture your charitie upon a boy.

Lan. Now, whats the matter? stand fast, and like your selfe.   *Isa.* Prethee no more wench.

Luce. What was his want to you.   *Isa.* Tis true.

Luce. Or misery, or say he had beene ith' Cage, was there no mercy to looke abroad but yours.

Isa. I am paid for fooling.

Luce. Must every slight companion that can purchase a shew of povertie and beggerly planet fall under your compassion.   *Lance.* Heres a new matter.

Luce. Nay you are served but too well, here he staies yet, yet as I live.   *Fran.* How her face alters on me?

Luce. Out of a confidence I hope.   *Isa.* I am glad ont.

Fran. How doe you gentle Lady?

Isa. Much ashamed sir, but first stand further off me y'are infectious to finde such vanitie, nay almost impudence where I beleeve a worth: is this your thankes, the gratitude you were so mad to make me, your trimme councell Gentlemen?

Lanc. What Lady?

Isa. Take your device agen, it will not serve sir, the woman will not bite, you are finely cosened, droppe it no more for shame.

Luce. Doe you thinke you are here sir amongst your wastcoateers, your base Wenches that scratch at such occasions; you are deluded; This is a Gentlewoman of a noble house, borne to a better fame than you can build her, and eyes above your pitch.   *Fran.* I doe acknowledge——

Isa. Then I beseech you sir, what could see, speake boldly, and speake truely, shame the devill, in my behaviour of such easinesse that you durst venture to doe this.

Fran. You amaze me, this Ring is none of mine, nor did I droppe it.   *Luce.* I saw you droppe it sir.

Isa. I tooke it up too, still looking when your modesty should misse it, why what a childish part was this?

Fran. I vow.

Isa. Vow me no vowes, he that dares doe this, has bred himselfe to boldnesse, to forsweare too; there take your gugaw you are too much pampered, and I repent my part, as

you

Wit without Money.

you grow older grow wiser if you can, and so farewell sir.
Exit Isabella and Luce.

Lan. Grow wiser if you can, shee has put it to you, tis a rich Ring, did you droppe it?

Fran. Never, nere see it afore *Lance*.

Lan. Thereby hangs a taile then: what slight shee makes to catch her selfe, looke up sir, you cannot lose her if you would, how daintily she flies upon the lure, and cunningly she makes her stoppes, whistle and she'le come to you.

Fran. I would I were so happie.

Lan. Maids are clockes, the greatest wheele they show, goes slowest to us, and makes hang on tedious hopes the lesser, which are concealed being often oyl'd with wishes flee like desires, and never leave that motion, till the tongue strikes; she is flesh, blood, and marrow, young as her purpose, and soft as pitty; no Monument to worship, but a mould to make men in, a neate one, and I know how ere she appeares now, which is neare enough, you are starke blinde if you hit not soone at night; shee would venture fortie pounds more but to feele a flea in your shape bite her: drop no more Rings forsooth, this was the prettiest thing to know her heart by.

Fran. Thou putst me in much comfort.

Lan. Put your selfe in good comfort, if shee doe not point you out the way, droppe no more rings, she'le droppe her selfe into you.

Fran. I wonder my brother comes not.

Lan. Let him alone, and feede your selfe on your owne fortunes; come be frolicke, and lets be monstrous wise and full of councell, droppe no more Ringes. *Exit.*

Enter Widdow, Fountaine, Bellamore, Harebraine.

Wid. If you will needes be foolish you must be used so: who sent for you? who entertained you Gentlemen? who bid you welcome hether? you came crowding, and impudently bold; presse on my patience, as if I kept a house for all Companions, and of all sorts; will 'have your wills, will 'vexe me and force my liking from you, I never owed you.

Fount. For all this we will dine with you.

Bell. And for all this will have a better answer from you.

Wid. You shall never, neither have a answer nor dinner,

Wit without Money.

unlesse you use me with a more staid respect, and stay your time too. *Enter Isabella, Shorthose, Roger, Humphrey, Ralph, with dishes of meate.*

Isa. Forward with the meate now.

Rog. Come gentlemen march fairely.

Short. Roger, you are a weake Servingman, your white broath runnes from you; fie, how I sweate under this pile of Beefe; an Elephant can doe more, oh for such a backe now, and in these times, what might a man arrive at; Goose grase you up, and Woodcocke march behinde thee, I am almost foundred.

Wid. Who bid you bring the meate yet? away you knaves, I will not dine these two houres, how am I vext and chafed; goe carry it backe and tell the Cooke, hee's an arrant Rascall, to send before I called.

Short. Faces about Gentlemen, beate a mournefull march then, and give some supporters, or else I perish. *Exeunt Servants.*

Isa. It does me much good to see her chafe thus.

Hare. Wee can stay Madame, and will stay and dwell here, tis good Ayre.

Foun. I know you have beds enough, and meate you never want. *Wid.* You want a little.

Bell. We dare to pretend on, since you are curlish, wee'le give you physicke, you must purge this anger, it burnes you and decaies you.

Wid. If I had you out once I would be at charge of a percullis for you. *Enter Vallantine.*

Val. Good morrow noble Lady.

Wid. Good morrow sir, how sweetly now he lookes, and how full manly, what slaves was these to use him so.

Val. I come to looke a young man I call brother.

Wid. Such a one was here sir, as I remember your owne brother, but gone almost an houre agoe.

Val. God e'n then.

Wid. You must not so soone sir, here be some Gentlemen, it may be you are acquainted with um.

Hare. Will nothing make him miserable?

Foun. How glorious!

R*ell*

Wit without Money.

Bell. It is the very he, does it raine fortunes, or has hee a familliar.

Hare. How doggedly he lookes too.

Foun. I am beyond my faith, pray lets be going.

Val. Where are these Gentlemen? *Wid.* Here.

Val. Yes I know um and will be more familier.

Bell. Morrow Maddam.

Wid. Nay stay and dine.

Val. You shall stay till I talke with you, and not dine neither, but fastingly my fury, you thinke you have undone me, thinke so still, and swallow that beleefe, till you be company for Court-hand Clarkes, and starved Atturneyes, till you breake in at playes like Prentises for three a groat, and cracke nuts with the scollers in penny Roomes agen, and fight for Apples, till you returne to what I found you, people betrai'd into the hands of Fencers, Challengers, Toothdrawers bills, and tedious Proclamations in Meale-markets, with throngings to see Cutpurses: stirre not, but heare, and marke, Ile cut your throates else, till Waterworkes, and rumours of new Rivers rid you againe and runne you into questions who built Thamea, till you runne mad for Lotteries, and stand there with your tables to gleane the golden sentenses, and cite um secretly to Servingmen for sound Essayes, till Tavernes allow you but a Towell roome to tipple in wine that the Bell hath gone for twice, and glasses that looke like broken promises, tied up with wicker protestations, English Tobacco with halfe pipes, nor in halfe a yeare once burnt, and Bisket that Bawdes have rubb'd their gummes upon like Curralls to bring the marke againe; tell these houre rascalls so, this most fatall houre will come againe, thinke I sit downe the looser.

Wid. Will you stay Gentlemen, a peece of beefe and a cold Capon, thats all, you know you are welcome.

Hum. That was cast to abuse us.

Bell. Steale off, the devill is in his anger.

Wid. Nay I am sure you will not leave me so discurteously now I have provided for you.

Val. What doe you heare? why doe vexe a woman of her goodnesse, her state and worth; can you bring a faire certificate

Wit without Money.

ficate that you deserve to be her footemen; husbands, you puppies, husbands for Whores and Bawdes, away you windsuckers; doe not looke bigge, nor prate, nor stay, nor grumble, and when you are gone seeme to laugh at my fury, and slight this Lady, I shall heare, and know this: and though I am not bound to fight for women, as farre as they are good I dare preserve um: be not too bold, for if you be Ile swinge you, Ile swinge you monstrously without all pittty, your honours now goe, avoide me mainely. *Exeunt.*

Wid. Well sir, you have delivered me, I thanke you, and with your noblenesse prevented danger their tongues might utter, will all goe and eate sir.

Val. No, no, I dare not trust my selfe with women, goe to your meate, eate little, take lesse ease, and tie your body to a daily labour, you may live honestly, and so I thank you. *Exit.*

Wid. Well goe thy wayes, thou art a noble fellow, and some meanes I must worke to have thee know it. *Exit.*

Actus 5. Scæn. 1.

Enter Uncle and Merchant.

Unc. MOst certaine tis, her hands that hold him up, and her sister relieves *Franke*.

Mer. I am glad to heare it: but wherefore doe they not pursue this fortune to some faire end?

Unc. The women are too craftie, *Vellantine* too coy, and *Franke* too bashfull, had any wise man hold of such a blessing, they would strick it out oth' flint but they would for me it. *Enter Widdow and Shorthose.*

Mer. The Widdow sure, why does shee stirre so earely.

Wid. Tis strange, I cannot force him to understand mee, and make a benefit, of what I would bring him, tell my sister ile use any devotions at home this morning, shee may if shee please goe to Church.

Short. Hay ho.

Wid. And doe you waite upon her with a torch sir?

Short. Hay ho.

Wid.

Wid. You lasie knave.

Short. Here is such a single ranklings that we can nere lie quiet, and sleepe our prayers out, *Ralph* pray emptie my night shooe that you made your Chamberpot, and burne a little Rosemary int, I must waite upon my Lady, This morning Prayer has brought me into a consumption, I have nothing left but flesh and bones about me.

Wid. You drousie slave, nothing but sleepe and swilling.

Short. Had you beene bitten with bandogge fleaes, as I have beene, and haunted with the night Mare.

Wid. With an Alepot.

Short. You would have little list to morning Prayers, pray take my fellow *Ralph*, hee has a Psalme booke, I am an ingrum man.

Short. Get you ready quickly, and when she is ready waite upon her hansomely; no more, be gone.

Short. If I doe snore my part out———   *Exit Short.*

Vnc. Now to our purposes.

Mer. Good morrow Madam.

Wid. Good morrow Gentlemen.

Vnc. Good joy aud fortune.

Wid. These are good things, and worth my thankes, I thanke you sir.

Mer. Much joy I hope you'le finde, we came to gratulate your new knit marriage band.

Wid. How?

Vnc. Hes a Gentleman although he be my kinsman, my faire Neece.

Wid. Neece Sir?

Vnc. Yes Lady, now I may say so, tis no shame to you, I say a Gentleman, and winking at some light fancies, which you most happily may affect him for, as bravely carried, as nobly bred and managed.

Wid. Whats all this, I understand you not, what Neece, what marriage knot.

Vnc. Ile tell plainely, you are my Neece, and *Vallentine* the Gentleman has made you so by marriage.

Wid. Marriage?

H 2   *Vnc.*

Wit without Money.

Unc. Yes Lady, and twas a noble and a vertuous part, to take a falling man to your protection, and bay him up againe to all his glories.

Wid. The men are mad.

Mer. What though he wanted these outward things, that flie away like shadowes; was not his minde a full one, and a brave one, you have wealth enough to give him glosse, and outside; and he wit enough to give way to love a Lady.

Unc. I ever thought he would doe well.

Mer. Nay, I knew how ever he wheel'd about like a loose Cabine, he would charge home at length, like a brave Gentleman, heavens blessing a'your heart Lady, wee are so bound to honour you, in all your service so devoted to you.

Unc. Doe not looke so strange Widdow it must be knowne, better a generall joy; no stirring here yet, come, come you cannot hide um.

Wid. Pray be not impudent, these are the finest toyes, be-like I am married then.

Mer. You are in a miserable estate in the worlds account else, I would not for your wealth it come to doubting.

Wid. And I am great with child?

Unc. No; great they say not, but tis a full opinion you are with childe, and great joy among the Gentlemen, your husband hath bestirred himselfe fairely.

Mer. Alas, we know his private houres of entrance, how long, and when he staied, could name the bed too where hee paid downe his first fruits.

Wid. I shall beleeve anon.

Unc. And we consider for some private reasons, you would have it private, yet take your owne pleasure; and so good morrow my best Neece, my sweetest.

Wid. No, no; pray stay.

Unc. I know you would be with him, love him, and love him well.

Mer. You'le finde him noble, this may beget——

Unc. It must needes work upon her. *Exit Unc. & Mer.*

Wid. These are fine bobes I faith, married, and with child too, how long has this beene I trow? they seeme grave fellowes,

lowes, they should not come to flour, married, and bedded, the world take notice too, where lies this May game, I could be vext extreamely now, and raile too, but tis to no end, though I itch little, must I be scratch'd I know not how, who waites there?

Enter Hum, a servant.

Hum. Madam.

Wid. Make ready my Coach quickly, and waite you onely, and harke you sir, be secret and speedy, enquire out where he lies.

Hum. I shall doe it Madam. *Exit*

Wid. Married, and got with child in a dreame, tis fine ifaith, sure he that did this, would doe better waking. *Exit*

Enter Vallentine, Fran. Lance, and a boy with a torch.

Val. Hold thy Torch hansomely, how dost thou *Francke*, *Peter Bassell*, beare up.

Fran. You have fryed me soundly, Sacke doe you call this drinke.

Val. A shrewd dogge *Francke*, will bite abundantly.

Lan. Now could I fight, and fight with thee.

Val. With me thou man of *Memphis*.

Lan. But that thou art mine owne naturall Master, yet my sackes saies thou art no man, thou art a Pagan, and pawnest thy land, which a noble cause?

Val. No armes, no armes, good *Lancelet*, deare *Lance*, no fighting here, we will have Lands boy, Livings, and Titles, thou shalt be a Viceroy, hang fighting, hang tis out of fashion.

Lan. I would faine labour you into your lands againe, goe too, it is behoovefull.

Fran. Fie *Lance*, fie.

Lan. I must beate some body, and why not my Master, before stranger, charity and beating begins at home.

Val. Come thou shalt beate me.

Lan. I will not be compeld, and you were two Masters, I scorne the motion.

Val. Wilt thou sleepe.

Lan. I scorne sleepe.

Val. Wilt thou goe eate.

Lan. I scorne meate, I come for rompering, I come to write

H 3 upon

Wit without Money

upon my charge discreetly, for looke you, if you will not take your Mortgage againe, here doe I lie Saint *George*, and so forth.

Val. And here doe I St. *George*, bestride the Dragon, thus with my Lance.

Lan. I sting, I sting with my taile.

Val. Doe you so, doe you so Sir, I shall taile you presently.

Fran. By no meanes doe not hurt him.

Val. Take his Nellson, and now rise thou maiden Knight of Malligo, lace on thy helmet of inchanted sacke, and charge againe.

Lan. I play no more, you abuse me, will you goe.

Fran. Ile bid you good morrow Brother, for sleepe I cannot I have a thousand fancies.

Val. Now thou art arived, goe bravely to the matter, and doe something of worth *Francke*.

Lan. You shall heare from us.   *Exit Lance and Franke.*

Val. This rogue, if he had beene sober, sure had beaten me, is the most tettish knave.

Enter Vncle and Merchant, May. with a torch.

Vnc. Tis he.

Mer. Good morrow.

Val. Why sir good morrow to you too, and you be so lusty

Vnc. You have made your brother a fine man, we met him.

Val. I made him a fine Gentleman, he was a foole before, brought up amongst the midst of small beere Brue-houses, what would you have with me.

Mer. I come to tell you, your latest houre is come.

Val. Are you my sentence.

Mer. The sentence of your state.

Val. Let it be hang'd then, and let it be hang'd hie enough, I may not see it.

Vnc. A gracious resolution.

Val. What would you else with me, will you goe drinke, and let the world slide Vncle, ha, ha, ha, boyes, drinke sacke like whey boyes.

Mer. Have you no feeling sir.

Val. Come hither Merchant, Make me a supper, thou most
reverent

Wit without Money.

reverent Land catcher, a supper of forty pound.

Mer. What then sir.

Val. Then bring thy wife along, and thy faire sisters, thy neighbours and their wives, and all their trinkets, let me have forty trumpets, and such wine, weele laugh at all the miseries of morgage, and then in state Ile render thee an answer.

Mer. What say to this.

Unc. I dare not say nor thinke neither.

Mer. Will you redeeme your state, speake to the point sir.

Val. Not, not if it were mine heire in the Turkes gallies.

Mer. Then I must take an order.

Val. Take a thousand, I will not keepe it, nor thou shalt not have it, because thou camest ith nick, thou shalt not have it, goe take possession, and be sure you hold it, hold fast with both hands, for there be those hounds uncoupled, will ring you such a knell, goe downe in glory, and march upon my Land, and cry alls mine, cry as the devil did, and be the devill, marke what an eccho followes, build fine Marchpanes, to entertaine Sir Silkeworme and his Lady, and pull the Chappell downe, to raise a Chamber for Mistris Silverpin, to lay her belly in, marke what an Earthquake comes, then foolish Merchant my tennants are no subjects, they obey nothing, and they are people too, never Christned, they know no law, nor conscience, theile devoure thee : and thou mortall the stople, theile confound thee, within three dayes; no bit nor memory of what thou wert, no not the wart upon thy nose there, shall be ere heard of more, goe take possession, and bring thy children downe, to rost like rabbits, they love young toasts, and butter, Bowbell suckers as they love mischiefe, and hate law, they are Canibals: bring downe thy kindred too, that be not fruitfull, there be those Mandrakes, that will mollifie um, goe take possession, Ile goe to my Chamber, afore boy goe. *Exeu.*

Mer. Hees mad sure.

Unc. Hees halfe drunkē sure, and yet I like this unwillingnesse to loose it, this looking backe.

Mer. Yes if he did it hansomely, but hees so harsh, & strange

Unc. Beleeve it tis his drinke sir, and I am glad his drinke has thrust it out.

Mer.

Wit without Money.

Mer. Cannibals, if ever I come to view his regements, if faire termes may be had.

Vnc. Hee tels you true sir; They are a bunch of the most boystrous rascalls disorder ever made, let um be mad once, the power of the whole Country cannot coole um, be patient but a while.

Mer. As long as you will sir, before I buy a bargaine of such runts, Ile buy a Colledge for Beares, and live among um.

Enter Franscisco, Lance, boy with a torch.

Fran. How dost thou now.

Lan. Better then I was, and straighter, but my heads a hogs-head still, it rowles and tumbles.

Fran. Thou wert cruelly paid.

Lan. I may live to requite it, put a snaffle of sacke in my mouth, and then ride me very well.

Fran. Twas all but sport, Ile tell thee what I meane now, I meane to see this wench.

Lan. Where a devill is shee, and there were two, 'tweare better.

Fran. Dost thou heare the bell ring.

Lan. Yes, yes.

Fran. Then shee comes to prayers, earely each morning thether: Now if I could but meete her, for I am of another mettle now.

Enter Isabell, and Shorthose with a Torch.

Lan. What lights yond.

Fran. Ha, tis a light, take her by the hand and Court her.

Lan. Take her below the girdle, youle never speed else, it comes on this way still, oh that I had but such an opportunity in a saw pit, how it comes on, comes on, tis here.

Fran. Tis she, fortune I kisse thy hand ——— good morrow Lady.

Isa. What voyce is that sirrha, doe you sleepe as you goe, tis he, I am glad ont, why *Shorthose.*

Short. Yes forsooth, I was dreamt, I was going to Church.

Lan. Shee sees you as plaine as I doe.

Isa. Hold thy Torch up.

Short. Heres nothing but a stall, and a Butchers dogge a
sleepe

Wit without Money.

sleepe int, where did you see the voyce.

Fran. Shee lookes still angry.

Lan. To her and meet sir.

Isa. Here, here.

Fran. Yes Lady, never blesse your selfe, I am but a man, and like an honest man, now I will thanke you——

Isa. What do you meane, who sent for you, who desired you

Short. Shall I put out the Torch forsooth.

Isa. Can I not goe about my private meditations, hay, but such companions as you must ruffle me, you had best goe with me sir.

Fran. Twas my purpose.

Isa. Why what an impudence is this, you had best, being so neare the Church, provide a Priest, and perswade me to marry you.

Fran. It was my meaning, and such a husband, so loving, and so carefull, my youth, and all my fortunes shall arrive at —— Harke you.

Isa. Tis strange you should be thus unmannerly, turne home againe sirrah, you had best now force my man to leade your way.

Lan. Yes marry shall a Lady, forward my friend.

Isa. This is a pretty Riot, it may grow to a rape.

Fran. Doe you like that better, I can ravish you an hundred times, and never hurt you.

Short. I see nothing, I am asleepe still, when you have done tell me, and then Ile wake Mistris.

Isa. Are you in earnest Sir, doe you long to be hang'd.

Fran. Yes by my troth Lady in these faire tresses.

Isa. Shall I call out for helpe.

Fran. No by no meanes, that were a weake tricke Lady, Ile kisse and stoppe your mouth.

Isa. Youle answer all these.

Fran. A thousand kisses more.

Isa. I was never abused thus, you had best give out too, that you found me willing, and say I doted on you.

Fran. Thats knowne already, and no man living shall now carry you from me.

I

Isa.

Isa. This is fine ifaith.

Fran. It shall be tenne times finer.

Isa. Well seeing you are so valiant, keepe your way, I will to Church.

Fran. And I will waite upon you.

Isa. And it is most likely theres a Priest, if you dare venter as you professe, I would wish you looke about you, to doe these rude trickes, for you know their recompences, and trust not to my mercy.

Fran. But I will Lady.

Isa. For Ile so handle you.

Fran. Thats it I looke for.

Lan. Afore thou dreame.

Short. Have you done.

Isa. Goe on sir, and follow if you dare.

Fran. If I doe not hang me.

Lan. Tis all thine owne boy, an 'twere a million, god a mercy Sacke, when would small Beere have done this. *Exeunt.*

Knocking within.   *Enter Vallentine.*

Val. Whose that that knockes and bounces, what a devill ailes you, is hell broke loose, or doe you keepe an Iron mill.

Enter a servant.

Ser. Tis a Gentlewoman sir that must needs speak with you.

Val. A Gentlewoman, what Gentlewoman, what have I to doe with Gentlewomen?

Ser. She will not be answerd Sir.

Val. Fling up the bed and let her in, Ile try how gentle she is------ *Exit Servant.* This sacke has fild my head so full of bables, I am almost mad; what Gentlewoman should this be, I hope she has brought me no butter print along with her to lay to my charge, if she have tis all one, Ile forsweare it.

Enter Widdow.

Wid. O your a noble gallant, send of your servant pray.

Exit Servant.

Val. Shee will not ravish mee, by this light shee lookes as sharpe set as a Sparrow hawke, what wouldst thou woman.

Wid. O you have used me kindely, and like a Gentleman, this tis to trust to you.

Val.

Val. Trust to me, for what.

Wid. Because I said in jeast once, you were a hansome man, one I could like well, and fooling, made you beleeve I loved you, and might be brought to marry.

Val. The Widdow is drunke too.

Wid. You out of this which is a fine discretion, give out the matters done, you have wonne and wed mee, and that you have put fairely for an heire too, these are fine rumours to advance my credit; ith name of mischiefe what did you meane.

Val. That you loved me, and that you might be brought to marry me, why, what a devill doe you meane Widdow.

Wid. Twas a fine tricke too, to tell the world though you had enjoyed your first wish, you wished the wealth you aimed at; that I was poore, which is most true, I am, have sold my Lands, because I love not those vexations, yet for mine honors sake, if you must be prating, and for my credits sake in the Towne.

Val. I tell thee Widdow, I like thee ten times better, now thou hast no Lands, for now thy hopes and cares, lye on thy husband, if ere thou marryest more.

Wid. Have not you married me, and for this maine cause, now as you report it, to be your Nurse.

Val. My Nurse, why what am I growne too, give me the glasse, my Nurse.

Wid. You nere said truer, I must confesse I did a little favour you, and with some labour, might have beene perswaded, but when I found I must bee hourely troubled, with making brawthes, and dawbing your decaies with swadling, and with stitching up your ruines, for the world so reports.

Val. Doe not provoke me.

Wid. And halfe an eye may see.

Val. Doe not provoke me, the worlds a lying world, and thou shalt finde it, have a good heart, and take a strong faith to thee, and marke what followes, my Nurse, yes, you shall rocke me: Widdow Ile keepe you waking.

Wid. You are disposed sir.

Val. Yes marry am I Widdow, and you shall feele it, nay and they touch my freehold, I am a Tiger.

Wit without Money.

Wid. I thinke so.
Val. Come.
Wid. Whether.
Val. Any whether. *Sings.*

    The fits upon me now, the fits upon me now,
    Come quickely gentle Lady, the fits upon me now,
    The world shall know they are fooles,
    And so shalt thou doe too,
    Let the Cobler meddle with his tooles,
    The fits upon me now.

Take me quickly while I am in this vaine, away with me, for if I have but two houres to consider, all the Widdowes in the world cannot recover me.

Wid. If you will, goe with me sir.

Val. Yes marry will I, but tis in anger yet, and I will marry thee, doe not crosse me; yes, and I will lie with thee, and get a whole bundle of babies, and I will kisse thee, stand still and kisse me hansomely, but do not provoke me, stirre neither hand nor foote, for I am dangerous, I drunk sacke yesternight, doe not allure me: Thou art no widdow of this world, come in pitty, and in spite Ile marry thee, not a word more, and I may be brought to love thee. *Exeunt.*

Enter Merchant and Vncle at severall doores.

Mer. Well met agen, and what good newes yet.
Vnc. Faith nothing.
Mer. No fruites of what we sowed.
Vnc. Nothing I heare of.
Mer. No turning in this tide yet.
Vnc. Tis all flood, and till that fall away, theres no expecting.

Enter Fran. Isab. Lance, Shorthose, a torch.

Mer. Is not this his younger brother.
Vnc. With a Gentlewoman the Widdowes sister, as I live he smiles, he has got good hold, why well said *Francke* ifaith, lets stay and marke.

Isa. Well you are the prettiest youth, and so you have handled me, thinke you ha me sure.

Fran. As sure as wedlocke.

Isa.

Wit without Money.

Isa. You had best lye with me too.
Fran. Yes indeed will I, and get such blacke ey'd boyes.
Vnc. God a mercy *Francke*.
Isa. This is a merry world, poore simple Gentlewomen that thinke no harme, cannot walke about their businesse, but they must be catcht up I know not how.
Fran. Ile tell you, and Ile instruct you too, have I caught you Mistresse.
Isa. Well, and it were not for pure pitty, I would give you the slip yet, but being as it is.
Fran. It shall be better.

Enter Vallentine, Widdow, and Ralph with a Torch.

Isa. My sister as I live, your brother with her, sure I thinke you are the Kings takers.
Vnc. Now it workes.
Val. Nay you shall know I am a man.
Wid. I thinke so.
Val. And such proofe you shall have.
Wid. I pray speake softly.
Val. Ile speake it out Widdow, yes and you shall confesse too, I am no nurse child, I went for a man, a good one, if you can beate me out oth' pit.
Wid. I did but jest with you.
Val. Ile handle you in earnest, and so handle you: Nay when my credit cals.
Wid. Are you mad.
Val. I am mad, I am mad.
Fran. Good morrow Sir, I like your preparation.
Val. Thou hast beene at it *Francke*.
Fran. Yes faith, tis done sir,
Val. A long with me then, never hang an arse Widdow.
Isa. Tis to no purpose sister.
Val. Well said blackebrowes, advance your Torches Gentlemen.
Vnc. Yes, yes sir.
Val. And keepe your ranckes.
Mer. Lance carry this before him.
Vnc. Carry it in state.

I 3 *Enter*

Wit without Money.

Enter Musitians, Fount, Hare, Bell.

Val. What are you Musitians, I know your comming, and what are those behinde you.

Mus. Gentlemen that sent us to give the Lady a good morrow.

Val. O I know them, come boy sing the song I taught you, And sing it lustily, come forward Gentlemen, your welcome, Welcome, now we are all friends, goe get the Priest ready, And let him not be long, we have much businesse: Come *Francke* rejoyce with me, thou hast got the start boy, But ile so tumble after, come my friends leade, Lead chearefully, and let your fiddles ring boyes, My follies and my fancies have an end here, Display the morgage *Lance*, Merchant ile pay you, And every thing shall be in joynt agen.

Vnc. A fore, afore.

Val. And now confesse, and know. Wit without Money, sometimes gives the blow.

Exeunt.

FINIS.